Osprey Summer

A Very American Experience

BY THE SAME AUTHOR

Dolphins Under My Bed
The first stage of a journey that became the adventure of a lifetime

Turtles In Our Wake
Exploring some of the Mediterranean's loveliest islands

A Thousand Miles From Anywhere
Crossing the Atlantic to the Caribbean

---oOo---

There is in many of us the desire for a little adventure before it gets too late. David and Sandra Clayton decided to give up the security of home and jobs and turn a daydream into a reality. In this fourth book in the *Voyager* series they take the reader through the scenic beauty and captivating wildlife of America's Atlantic coast.

Reviews of earlier *Voyager* books:

'...superb storytelling style...' *Good Old Boat*

'...her ability to see the humor even in everyday situations will keep you laughing...' *Cruising World*

'Sandra Clayton writes so entertainingly.' *Ocean Cruising Club*

'...highly enjoyable reading.' Midwest Book Review

Website: https://sites.google.com/site/sandraclaytonauthor/

Sandra Clayton

Osprey Summer

A Very American Experience

Malvern Partnership

Published by Malvern Partnership
PO Box No 162, Heber City, Utah, 84032, USA

Copyright © Sandra Clayton 2014
First edition published 2014

ISBN: 978-0-9915904-0-7

Maps: Copyright ©David Clayton

Cover photograph: Thomas Point Shoal Light, Chesapeake Bay, Maryland. Copyright © Sandra Clayton.

Disclaimer:
This book is an account of a journey undertaken at a particular time and not in any way intended as a guide or aid to navigation. Nor should it be considered as a recommendation of any particular place or destination. The names and identifying details of individuals and vessels have often been changed to protect people's privacy.

CONTENTS

Florida to Virginia

Virginia to New Jersey

New Jersey to Massachusetts

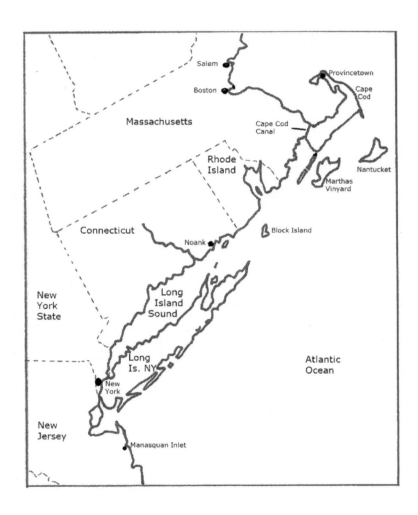

Acknowledgements

Voyager's crew would like to express its gratitude for the following:

Atlantic Coast, Second Edition, published by MAPTECH, Inc
Cruising Association
Guide to Cruising Chesapeake Bay, 2000 Edition, Chesapeake Communications Inc.
Maptech Chartkits, Regions 2, 3 and 4.
Peterson Field Guides – Eastern Birds by Roger Tory Peterson, published by Houghton Mifflin Company
Reeds Nautical Almanac: North American East Coast published by Adlard Coles Nautical
Royal Yachting Association
The late Skipper Bob and his *Anchorages Along The Intracoastal Waterway*
The Atlantic Crossing Guide published by Adlard Coles Nautical, 4th edition
The Intracoastal Waterway Chartbook, Third Edition, published by International Marine, a Division of the McGraw-Hill Companies
United States Army Corps of Engineers

Also to Island Press, Washington, DC for permission to reproduce material from: *Alone* by Admiral Richard E. Byrd. Copyright © 1938 Richard E. Byrd, renewed 1966 by Marie A. Byrd.

About Voyager

Voyager is a heavy cruising catamaran that was built by Solaris Yachts at Southampton. They built strong, comfortable boats but ceased trading after a disastrous fire spread from a neighbouring yard. *Voyager* is their Sunstream model, 40 ft long x 16 ft wide with twin 27hp diesel engines.

She is a typical British catamaran in that she has a small mainsail and a large genoa which is her main source of power. She is cutter rigged and therefore has a small staysail.

Her two hulls are connected by a bridge deck with a cabin on it which provides the main living area, or saloon. It contains a large sofa, a coffee table, a dining table and a chart table. Opposite the chart table, and overlooking the galley, the starboard dining seating quickly converts to a breakfast bar which also makes an ideal dining area for any meal on a bouncy sea as there is less potential for loose objects to move about.

From the saloon, you enter the starboard or right-hand hull down three steps. Immediately in front of you is the galley. Turn right and there is an additional food preparation area, storage for cutlery and crockery and a large chest refrigerator. In the stern is a double bunk, a wardrobe, dressing table and clothing cupboards. Underneath the bunk is one of *Voyager*'s engines. At the bow end of this hull there is a head containing a toilet, wash basin and a bath.

The port hull contains in its stern an identical suite to the one in the starboard hull plus a shower, toilet and vanity. There is a further cabin in the bow of this hull but for the voyage we converted it into a storage space with a small workbench and vice.

Out on deck *Voyager* has a deep, well protected cockpit and all her sails can be handled from within it.

Prelude

For many of us there comes a time when you want to make a change in your life, even though you might not know exactly what it is you want to do instead. You just know that you don't want to go on doing what you are currently doing for the foreseeable future. And for a while this discontent settles like a cloud overhead. Then the epiphany comes, the realization of what it is you really want.

Ours occurred one cold, damp winter's night. *What if,* David had said, *we sold the house and sailed off somewhere warm?* He could also have added *before we get too old*, but he didn't because we were already feeling pretty low.

To wait for the statutory retirement age of 65 would have meant, on our current showing, that when the time came we should not be up to the physical demands of blue water cruising. So we decided to bite the bullet of a reduced pension, sold our house in a recession and made our home on a forty-foot catamaran called *Voyager*.

The Mediterranean had been our first objective. Since then we have cruised the Atlantic islands of Madeira, the Canaries and Cape Verde, crossed the Atlantic, wintered in the Caribbean and are now hovering off America's Florida shore. We had never expected to cruise the USA, since any long-term use of American marinas put it entirely outside our price range. Until, that is, a chance conversation with a fellow yachtswoman in Antigua.

As a result of that encounter we are looking forward to a whole new experience. After nearly two years of coastal waters, island-hopping and some challenging offshore sailing we have before us over a thousand miles of inland waterway up America's eastern seaboard from Fort Lauderdale to Norfolk, Virginia. After that we have the option of mostly sheltered water from Norfolk to New York and beyond. And there are anchorages all the way.

Having spent time in quite a few countries by now, we are very aware of the difference between the reality and a second-hand view of them through films and books or, at best, a brief and untypical experience via a holiday resort.

We are therefore greatly looking forward to getting past the Hollywood, TV sitcom and news media images and discovering something a little closer to the real America. All we have to do now is complete the formalities and we are ready to begin.

FLORIDA

1
Fort Lauderdale

'I'm sorry,' the Immigration Officer says, 'but your visas are invalid.'

David and I have just spent ten turbulent days and nights crossing from the Virgin Islands to Fort Lauderdale through violent seas and unpredictable currents. There was also an electrical storm in the Bermuda Triangle which I hadn't expected to survive, and the Gulf Stream which had been so strong at times that it almost swept us away.

Having successfully landed on America's south-eastern shore, however, we have been anticipating a leisurely summer up its Intracoastal Waterway, or ICW for short. Cooler than the Caribbean. Sheltered from the unpredictable weather patterns of the past year. And protected from Atlantic rollers. A thousand miles of infinitely varied waterway that we have been anticipating ever since we were first told about it three months ago.

As yachtsmen are required to do, we have moored at a US Customs & Immigration-approved marina and telephoned their offices, hailed a taxi and fronted up at Immigration. We are second in line, behind a French couple with three children.

When you telephone in to advise of your arrival the person on the other end gives you a Customs clearance number to hand to Immigration and tells you that you have a maximum of 48 hours in which to clear in. *However*, it is *expected* that you will report in person at Immigration as soon as you have secured your boat.

When asked by the officer exactly *when* he had landed on US soil the Frenchman, in a Gallic, shoulder-shrugging, palms-upward sort of way, casually reveals that he has taken 48 hours as his starting point rather than an end point, having a look around first: at the beach, the shopping mall, the supermarket ... The shoulders lift again.

I find myself wondering whether he has come from France or from one of the Caribbean's French islands. Because, if he had sailed from as far away as Europe, something he would have learned by now is not to mess with immigration officials.

The one currently eyeballing him with the intensity of a laser beam is not best pleased. He is even less pleased to learn that the Frenchman has not seen fit to acquire visas for himself and his family to enter America.

The official is so irritated, in fact, that he tells the family to sit down and wait, and calls us to his counter instead.

We have sat quietly and, I am ashamed to say, a little smugly throughout this interview. We have not only reported in immediately on securing our boat, but possess lifetime visas. A decade ago we had applied for a visa each for a two-week holiday and been given six-month visas for life, as had been America's wont at that time.

The official asks when we had arrived in the country and where we are berthed. Our answers seem to satisfy him. Then, as requested, we hand over our passports. He opens them. And that's when he says, 'I'm sorry, but your visas are invalid.'

Sometimes it is hard to credit how fast a large amount of data can hurtle through your brain when you receive a shock. We shall have no alternative but to go back the way we have come. With less than four weeks to the hurricane season we shall have to return south, down the Caribbean island chain to Trinidad. It is now early May. We have only until the first day of June - the start of the hurricane season – to remove *Voyager* to a place of safety before our insurance company washes its hands of us.

Some yachtsmen remain in the hurricane zone uninsured. We recently met two who'd done it. Both had been hit in the sheltered anchorage of Simpson Bay Lagoon, on the Caribbean island of St Martin.

One of them told us that he'd spent three days under 100mph winds but his boat had survived. The other saw the family yacht destroyed. It is a risk we are not prepared to take.

Trinidad is below the hurricane belt. It will be something of a rush to get there, and not a particularly enjoyable passage given the erratic and often uncomfortable conditions we experienced getting here.

But there is another difficulty involved in going south. Heat. It has not been such a problem for David but I have found even the late spring temperatures of the northern Caribbean too much at times. The reason we have been glad to be heading up north out of the hurricane zone has been to avoid the kind of summer heat you get sixteen hundred miles to the south.

Our faces probably have on them that mortified stare of the small furry mammal caught in a car's headlights known as 'glazed rabbit' and familiar to immigration officials the world over.

It seems that the American government has recently changed its rules on visas. Unfortunately, when drawing up this new legislation, the lawmakers had had in mind only the vast proportion of people who enter the US, either as holidaymakers or on business, who travel on scheduled flights or shipping and stay for just a week or two. They had forgotten about yachtsmen. After patiently explaining this to us the official looks down at our own visas.

'I have to cancel these,' he says, inking a rubber stamp bearing the word *Cancelled* and lowering it onto them.

Our shoulders sag.

'But I shall give you temporary ones,' he adds. And, in a touch I really appreciate, across each of the two stamp marks saying *Cancelled* he writes neatly in ballpoint pen, 'without prejudice'. He then wields another rubber stamp allowing us entry for six months, but says if we want to come back in again we must have proper visas obtainable from the US embassy in our own country.

The normal fee for turning up without a visa or with an invalid one, he tells us, is $170 each. However, he intends to waive this fee in our case, 'as it is not your fault'.

We thank him very much. He smiles. But in the instant we turn away from his counter his face darkens, his attention now focused behind us, on the Frenchman.

'*Sir*,' he says in his direction, in a voice that lowers the temperature in the room by several degrees. We leave quickly.

We descend two floors to Customs, buy a cruising permit for $9 and emerge onto the wide Florida boulevard outside as bona fide visitors with six whole months ahead of us. In a burst of exuberance I leap to the kerb and flag down an oncoming taxi. It turns out to be the County Sheriff but he takes it well.

2
First Impressions

Every new country – even a different part of a large country - is a new experience. It looks, smells, sounds and feels different. You only have to look down at your feet, at what you're standing on. During the winter months this has included black and white mosaic pavements, cobbled streets, dirt roads and coral sand. Here in a Florida marina it is a kind of grass unlike any we've ever encountered before. Broad-bladed, thick and coarse, to withstand the Florida climate.

The raucous, shiny black birds with iridescent heads strutting about on it are not crows either, as a Briton might expect, but grackles. They sound like their name. They stamp about going, 'grack, grack, grack' and seem to ooze noise from every quill. Even their wings are audible when they fly. At the other extreme is the brown pelican. Maybe six times larger than the grackle, they make only one sound, 'Ha'. Loudly if annoyed. Softly when content. The rest is silence.

There is also the strange phenomenon of 'seeing' famous people. At least for me. It doesn't seem to affect David. But I turn my head, catch a glimpse and just for a moment... We are berthed in a large hotel and marina complex and to reach the main road from our slip we have to pass the doors of the hotel. A tall, rangy man with long wispy hair and beard emerges and for a second I think I have just seen Howard Hughes striding out of the lobby until I remember that he departed this life some time ago. Earlier it had been Andy Devine, on the opposite pontoon, off for a day's fishing and looking just like he did in the 1939 movie *Stagecoach*.

And, naturally, everything is big; from the buildings to the boats in the marina. And rich. The motor yacht behind us is so big it blocks out the sun until noon. It is washed from top to bottom every day, its two friendly cleaners tell us. They are migrants whose own country's economy recently and spectacularly collapsed and though well-educated and with professional qualifications they are cleaning boats to get by. The boat's owners are staying in the adjacent hotel and only go on board their mega yacht to use its Jacuzzi.

We go into town and visit Barnes and Noble, a bookshop as big as a department store. After so long afloat, much of it through countries where choice has been limited or English a foreign language, we are sorely in need of fresh reading matter. Unlike most places we've ever been, where someone begins to cough politely but insistently if you spend too long with your nose in one of their books, here they provide armchairs and coffee and the whole place has the air of a very comfortable lending library.

At Bluewater Books we buy charts for the ICW and a copy of Skipper Bob's *Anchorages Along the Intracoastal Waterway*, an A4 spiral-bound publication which lists anchorages, free moorings and cheap sources of diesel along its 1,243-mile length from Key West in Florida to Norfolk, Virginia. In terms of marine publications it is one of the best $14 we will ever spend.

Radio Shack sells us one of their inexpensive little weather radios. It will pick up a continuous forecast, for whichever area we are in, from the weather stations all the way along the coast.

A new kettle from a kitchenware store offers a lifetime guarantee. 'Who's lifetime?' I ask the shop assistant (sorry, associate). 'The product's,' she says, as if that should have been obvious to anyone. But while the warranty may be worthless the logic is unassailable.

And we visit a supermarket for a big shop up, since after ten days at sea our stores are running low. Two things in particular strike us. One is sheer variety. After months spent wandering around small Caribbean grocery shops trying to find a change from chicken, we are overwhelmed by a vast choice of meat, fish, poultry and seafood. Plus twenty-four different brands of biscuit, even if all of them are chocolate chip cookies.

Being presented with so many different types and combinations of yoghurt to choose from is bewildering. Cow's milk. Goat's milk. Cow's & goat's milk. Whole milk. Low fat, non-fat, cultured low fat, cultured dairy. Double protein. Organic. Plain, Greek style, Greek strained, Greek all natural. Fruit flavour. Real fruit pieces. Fruit on the bottom. And all involving more varieties of cherries and berries and assorted exotica than I ever knew existed. Then there's cheesecake flavour, black forest gateau, key lime pie and pina colada. But what finally stops me dead in my tracks is one labelled Brown Cow. 'Oh, no!' I wail. 'I don't have to choose the colour of the cow as well, do I?' But it turns out to be a trade name and I'm getting over-tired. David takes a couple of cartons off the shelf at random and steers me away.

The other startling thing, apart from choice, is politeness. Standing between two rows of shelves, gawping at a stupefying range of tinned red kidney beans, a woman wheels her shopping cart between me and the shelf in front of me. There is plenty of room in this wide-aisled, hangar-sized supermarket for her to pass easily but nevertheless she says softly, 'Excuse me.'

I assume it is sarcasm, for the thoughtless way I've plonked myself and my trolley in the middle of the aisle. But no, something similar happens soon after. While well used to having a trolley shoved into my heels or a thumb nail lunge inches from my eyeball to snatch a plastic bag off a roll, I have never before had a fellow shopper apologise for momentarily cutting off my view of a shelf. I am captivated.

I think along with 'big' and 'rich' a defining characteristic is politeness. People, we discover, are routinely polite. Not the snarling, 'Have a nice day!' beloved by film makers, but a genuine consideration for other people's comfort and welfare.

Finally our to-do list is complete but for one item. We have been unable to phone home since none of the American telephone companies will accept British credit cards; the marina will not agree to a collect call, and when we try to make one from a public phone box there is no reply.

We are also rather tired, say *hang the expense* and decide to stay another night. We shall be glad we did, for the following day has a pleasant surprise in store. It is a day of personal celebration but David isn't expecting a fuss. In fact, in recent years he has become increasingly loath to even acknowledge its existence. Nevertheless I am preparing a special lunch and he has just opened a decent bottle of wine when we become aware of a lot of activity in the sky above our heads.

'Wow!' I cry. 'They're putting on a flypast for your birthday!'

'Only in America,' he sighs appreciatively, raising his glass towards a vast array of bi-planes and stunt planes, B52 bombers, F111s, Tomcats and airships. There is also a stunning display by the Blue Angels, the US Navy's flight demonstration squadron and America's equivalent of the RAF's Red Arrows aerobatic team. Some fly in pairs, wing-tip to wing-tip and then in the blink of an eye one of them inverts and flies upside down, still wing-tip to wing-tip. It is breathtaking. The show even includes the ever-so-secret Stealth Bomber.

On a stroll along the beach later - with warships gathered offshore, servicemen and women on parade and the planes still flying overhead - we notice signs saying *Air Force and Navy Day* and *Salute to the Military Air & Sea Show* but consider the display above our cockpit to have been no less of a personal treat for that.

3
The ICW

We leave the marina after breakfast in a light easterly breeze on a fine May morning and glide past fabulous homes set among landscaped gardens and tall, waving palm trees. It is known locally, and with uncharacteristic understatement, as Millionaires Row since being a mere millionaire would not be enough to get you a house on this stretch of waterway. Some are so vast they seem to have more in common with convention centres than private homes and all of them have their own stretch of waterfront, enabling the family's boats to be moored on one side of the house while its cars are garaged on the other.

Normally houses have a main frontage, which is its public facade and seen from the road; and the back garden - or yard, as Americans prefer to call it - which is considered the private part of a home's exterior. Except that when you live on a busy waterfront the back of your house is as public as the front, with people forever overlooking your private pleasures.

A house also makes a statement about its owners but none more so than the one with an enormous statue – reaching above the roof line - of a hand giving the world the middle finger. Perhaps it is the aforementioned lack of privacy that the householder objects to. If so, as a deterrent to prying eyes the sculpture is an abject failure because the rails of passing boats are lined with people either pointing it out to their companions or aiming cameras at it.

One thing that surprises us is that not only are windows and doors screened against insects but also porches, patios, swimming pools and tennis courts. Everything open to the outside air, in fact, is cocooned in a fine black mesh that leaves you with an impression of the inhabitants imprisoned in a perpetual half-light. Another is that we never see any people out enjoying these lovely homes, only liveried young men from garden maintenance companies. Maybe the owners are simply out at work making the money to pay for it all.

We are currently en route to Lake Boca Raton. This will be our first anchorage on the Intracoastal Waterway, so called because it lies in between coast and mainland. There are actually three ICWs, two of which run along the Gulf coast. However, the one which has been singing its siren song to us in recent weeks is the Atlantic Intracoastal Waterway which lies inside the eastern seaboard between Florida's Key West and Norfolk, Virginia. From there we plan to enter Chesapeake Bay, one of America's premier sailing areas and somewhere David has been reading about for some time.

The ICW's system of rivers, lagoons, lakes and ocean inlets, connected where necessary by man-made canals, meanders for more than a thousand miles through the cities, towns, marshes, swamp, grasslands, fields, forest and peat bogs of five states - Florida, Georgia, South and North Carolina and Virginia - and is affectionately referred to by some of the boaters who frequent it as 'The Ditch'.

It is a unique opportunity to see inland America from the deck of an ocean-going yacht, although it is mostly a motoring waterway. There are a few open areas in which to sail, and if the wind happens to be in the right direction you can raise a sail on the rivers too. But a 27hp marine engine uses very little fuel, leaves a small carbon footprint and, in terms of expense, this journey was made at a time when diesel cost less than a dollar per US gallon.

Although Lake Boca Raton is only 18 miles away it is a slow journey because there are seven lifting bridges to get through. They are of the bascule type, where a section of the roadway rises like a drawbridge. Many of the ICW's bridges open on demand but whether they do or not depends on the importance of the roads passing over them in keeping traffic flowing. So the closer you are to a major city or freeway the more likely it is that bridges will open only at specific times.

All the bridges on this stretch of water open by the clock, because you can't have constant traffic snarl-ups in a high density area caused by boats turning up only minutes after a bridge has closed and asking for it be opened again. So if you have just missed an opening you may have to hover for half an hour until the next one. But you soon get into the rhythm of things and, since the times of all the bridge openings are listed in the book of charts and *Skipper Bob*, with a little thought it is usually possible to minimize the waiting time.

Lake Boca Raton is more like a large shallow pond than a lake and only deep enough for us to anchor in one corner, despite *Voyager*'s shallow draught. There are no other boats here and, surrounded as it is by apartment blocks, it looks so like a private stretch of water that we wonder if we should really be here at all. But nobody comes and tells us to move so we put up our awning and our feet, and with a glass of wine and a new book – and despite all the buildings – it really feels quite private. Its Spanish name translates as *mouth of the rat*. Why it is called that no-one seems to know.

We leave the anchorage just after seven next morning and are almost immediately confronted by Palmetto Park Road Bridge, our first that opens on demand. To get an opening you simply call up, on whatever VHF channel number *Skipper Bob* says, and request one. The men and women who operate these bridges are called tenders and are invariably polite and professional, making every effort to accommodate both road and water traffic with minimal delays.

As well as their politeness and patience, the bridge tenders charm us with their form of address. In Britain only those in the Royal or Merchant Navies, and usually with a large vessel under their command, are called *captain*. Anyone in charge of a British leisure boat is its *skipper*. Here, regardless of size of boat, gender or age (occasionally children will call up the bridge) everyone is addressed as 'Captain'.

4
Lake Worth

Our destination is Lake Worth, around 20 miles long but even at its greatest extent less than a mile wide. It is separated from the sea by a narrow strip of land eighteen miles long, which also happens to be the famous Palm Beach.

Its earliest settler is reputed to have been Augustus Lang. Accounts vary. Some describe him as a deserter from the Confederate Army who in 1863 travelled down the virtually unpopulated east Florida coast, discovered a tropical lake - later named Lake Worth - built himself a palmetto hut and waited for the Civil War to end. Others have him as a Southern sympathiser on the run from Northern forces after sabotaging lighthouses so that Confederate troops could slip through blockades in the darkness.

He is also credited with cutting a small inlet to provide access between the ocean and the lake. Today many yachtsmen make this inlet the start of their ICW journey because by entering here they avoid what some consider to be uninteresting residential areas (the waterfront houses now long since reduced from the grandeur of Millionaires Row to merely human scale); and slow progress through all the bridges, of which there are eleven today.

We, on the other hand, are happy to dawdle and gawp. One of the anticipated pleasures of this voyage was simply to be leisurely. The only pressure on us now is to be above 35˚ North - which is officially outside the Hurricane Zone - by the first day of June, which is when our insurance company says the hurricane season officially begins.

As today is Sunday there is a lot more water traffic than we have experienced so far and much of it is power boats. With their tendency to rush about, especially up and down the channels on either side of the anchorage, it gets quite rough at times but they all disappear by evening. Then a number of yachts arrive and anchor with us. Some of them will set off up the ICW tomorrow while others are making an ocean passage and have come in through the Lake Worth Inlet only to rest up for the night.

Monday brings us our first fixed-span bridge. The official lower limit for fixed bridges on the ICW gives a clearance of 65 feet although there are reports of some being below that. Even 65 feet is too low for large yachts and the water far too shallow in places to accommodate a deep keel. Since *Voyager* requires only a 53-foot clearance, and a three-foot draught, the waterway's limits are not a problem for us.

An hour and a half after setting out we anchor at the far end of Lake Worth and dinghy to where there is a supermarket with a public telephone. To get ashore you pull your dinghy up onto a tiny triangle of sand beside a low bridge. Then you clamber over the railings and onto the road with clammy feet inside your deck shoes because you didn't prepare for wading ashore by bringing a towel. It is only a short walk to the store, however, and David ⸺⸺⸺⸺ h to his brother in England on a collect call, to tell h⸺ ⸺e and safely arrived in America.

It is an open-air ⸺ of the stanchions supporting the roof over a long, ⸺ ony running the length of the supermarket. While ⸺ other (who is convinced that we are victims-of-viole⸺ ⸺ my elbows on the rail and gaze out on a flat expans⸺ ⸺rida ⸺ shimmering in the early-morning heat, and recall the ⸺ green leaves nd white hawthorn blossoms of the soft English May ⸺ which ⸺ our house for the last time.

Inside the buil⸺g ⸺ an American checkout, it still comes as a surpris⸺ when the cashier calls someone over to bag your groceries for you w⸺ you ju⸺ re and watch. After a lifetime of bagging your own it ⸺ decadent somehow.

To add to our e⸺ ⸺ ⸺orth has the oldest baggers we have ever seen. The ⸺ ge⸺ ⸺ ⸺ his 70s, several seem to be in their mid-eighties w⸺ ⸺ ou's ⸺ a day. And these senior citizens are pushing shoppin⸺ ⸺ s of people young enough to be their great-grandchi⸺ren.

'It's OK,' we tell ⸺ to wheel our few purchases out of the air-conditioni⸺ an⸺ ⸺ pite the early hour, is already a white-hot parking ⸺ a car.' He frowns at us, uncomprehending. ⸺ ⸺orld, only people at the very bottom of the socio⸺onomic scale do⸺t have a car and we don't look shabby enough to be ⸺ those.

We will ask som⸺ ⸺ater wh⸺ ⸺da's supermarkets attract such elderly employees. ⸺een ⸺at ur⸺ European countries where a pension is for life, s⸺ ⸺ Americ⸺ p⸺ns⸺ns are for a limited number of years only. So if you ⸺ ⸺our p⸺nsio⸺ - and the climate here is noted for easing the joints ⸺d prom⸺ ⸺vity - you may spend your final years supporting yourself packing groceries at the local supermarket. Long a magnet for retirees from colder climes, with America's talent for snappy one-liners and *bon mots* it was inevitable that Florida would acquire the soubriquet *God's Waiting Room*.

Mid-morning we leave the lake and the suburban environment behind and enter a different landscape altogether: marshland, trees and waving grass. From here we make our way down a long narrow creek and enter Jupiter Sound, then Hobie Sound, both of them long narrow lakes, and on to St Lucie Inlet, a large estuary of sandbanks with a very narrow channel dredged across it to allow boats like ours to get into the Indian River.

5
Indian River

I think the Indian River is one of those places that will remain with me forever. Certain types of travel bring you face-to-face with cliché. Sailing along this waterway is one of them because this is the southern Florida coast, famously home to *CSI: Miami* and *Miami Vice*. Urban crime. High-rise apartment buildings. Concrete and tarmac. Urban sprawl. Multi-lane highways lined with used-car lots, advertisement hoardings and fast-food franchises, so that every town you drive through is a replica of the one you just left. Yet a mere 76 miles from the major conurbation of Fort Lauderdale is the start of the Indian River and you enter another world. It begins at the St Lucie ocean inlet and is 120 miles long.

Originally named Rio de Ais, after the tribe which once lived along it, this river is wider than most of the lakes we shall pass through, but so shallow outside the dredged channel that it is initially quite startling to see men in waders standing in it - wielding nets and fishing poles - half a mile or more from the shore.

In places it is littered with tiny islands, mostly with a tree or two on them. Its banks are wooded and the birdlife breathtaking. Roseate tern, piping plover, wood stork, bald eagle; brown pelicans by the hundred and a few of the rarer white; cormorants, large grey herons and their smaller blue relatives; duck and teal. And egrets in such vast numbers that when they roost, as they habitually do with their backs to the sun, they turn their host trees snowy white.

This bounty is helped by the fact that a number of wildlife refuges have been established along the river's length. The earliest of them, Pelican Island which we shall pass tomorrow, was initiated by a German immigrant called Paul Kroegel who moved to Florida in 1881 and whose home overlooked the island.

Appalled by the slaughter of pelicans, herons and egrets by plume hunters he sailed to the island and stood guard there. His continued efforts, along with those of several naturalists, resulted in the President being petitioned and in 1903 Theodore Roosevelt signed an executive order setting aside the three-acre island as a wildlife refuge in perpetuity - America's first federal bird reservation. Ironically, whole species were ultimately saved when women stopped wearing hats and caused the trade in exotic feathers to disappear.

We have travelled 43 miles today, the final one with less than three feet under our keel. Our home for the night is Big Mud Creek, reached by a narrow channel off the river. It lies in the shadow of a power station whose cooling system pumps warm water into the anchorage. And since warm water and soft mud are just the things to attract the comfort-loving manatee, this is a recognised place for a sighting. Unfortunately we run aground on a mud bank and have to rev our way off just when we are supposed to avoid disturbing any resident manatees.

According to our sea mammal book they are gentle, appealing creatures, vegetarian sea cows and distantly related to elephants, whose idea of high living is to lie undisturbed on the bottom of a warm lake or slow-moving river. The average adult manatee is about 10 feet long and weighs between 800 and 1200 pounds.

They live off sea grass and traditionally return to the same places and use the same rubbing stones every year. However, it seems that many manatees now find the annual migration back to the Bahamas an unnecessary exertion and remain in Florida all year round. Apart from boat propellers, the biggest threat to them is a drop in temperature. They cannot survive if the water drops below 65°F.

We leave Big Mud Creek at 7am with still no sign of one. Back out on the Indian River, beyond the dredged channel, men are already out in their waders.

Nine miles into today's passage we reach the Fort Pierce North Bridge, our only opening bridge of the day, all the others being fixed. I have already mentioned the good nature of the people tending these bridges but the one on duty here today might even have been the instrument of divine intervention for one mature jogger.

As we hover, waiting for the bridge to open, the warning bells clang, the street barriers come down and the vehicles at either end of the bridge grind to a halt. Perhaps the blood is roaring in his ears, or that mist which sometimes comes with over-exertion has formed before his eyes, but the grey-haired jogger, in shorts and sweatband, fails to notice that the traffic alongside him has disappeared.

At the centre of the bridge's lifting section he staggers to a halt and droops against the parapet, oblivious of the half dozen cars and trucks waiting at either end of the bridge, or of the hovering catamaran below him. Since nothing can move until the jogger does, the bridge tender hails him; but for some reason his public address system magnifies his words to an inordinate degree while at the same time slowing them down.

The effect is like the voice of God booming, 'YOU ... HAVE ... TO ... KEEP ... GOING!' At just this moment the rising sun breaks through a gap in the overcast sky, bathing the jogger in a shaft of golden light. He lifts his perspiring head, straightens, breaks into a determined if slightly unsteady run and clears the bridge. Then, like a man inspired, instead of doubling up again and resuming his panting, with his head high he just keeps on going.

The ICW has a dredged channel through it wherever its water is particularly shallow, and this channel has markers on either side of it. They consist of a sturdy wooden pile with either two red triangles or two green squares attached to it so that these port and starboard symbols can be easily seen from boats sailing in either direction.

Leisure boaters are not allowed to navigate the ICW during the hours of darkness but commercial vessels can, so at regular intervals along its length one of the markers is illuminated at night. This is achieved by fixing a small platform onto the top of the wooden pile just big enough to hold a battery and a light bulb in between the two marker panels.

Also stuffed between many of these double sets of port or starboard marker panels is a straggly nest although, built by what, we have no idea. However, by mid afternoon, in a very narrow stretch of channel, our starboard beam is only a foot or so away from one of these disreputable-looking nests and we finally get to see what inhabits them.

Osprey. A bird so endangered in the British Isles that for as long as I can remember the few surviving nesting sites, in very tall trees in the Scottish Highlands, have been protected by barbed wire and guarded by volunteers in a bid to foil egg collectors and prevent the species from dying out in Britain altogether. Imagine the delight, then, of looking down onto the back of a nesting osprey!

Although quite large in beak and claw, as well as body, the osprey proves to be a timid bird and this one flies off the nest; although circling and returning only moments after our boat has drifted on. And so we learn to be quiet as we approach these nests-on-stilts because it is not the boat or its closeness that bothers the birds but people moving and talking and waving their arms and cameras about, so we stay very still and quiet as we pass each nest and are soon rewarded by something we really never did expect to see.

Osprey, we quickly discover, are devoted parents, the males tirelessly supporting the females and chicks, and the next inhabited nest we pass has both parents standing on facing green marker boards and looking down at their fluffy bundle of joy. Except the little wretch clearly feels deprived in some way and is throwing an epic tantrum. It puts to shame the sort you sometimes see in the supermarket where a two-year-old turns on a full heel-drumming, back-arching, guilt-inducing performance in pursuit of something sweet and sticky.

This tiny starter kit of bone and feathers is *furious*, shrieking its head off, jumping up and down and waving its stubby little wings at two devastated adults who, in the moments that it takes our boat to pass them, look up at us with an expression that can only be described as utter dismay. Then they look briefly into each other's bewildered eyes and back down helplessly at the angry, leaping, scrawny-necked little creature that they have so recently and so lovingly ushered into the world. From their obvious distress, one can only assume that they are first-time parents.

We are also visited by dolphins during the day, some of them swimming in pairs like courting couples in the spring sunshine, others gathering in small gangs under bridges and eyeing up our boat as a source of entertainment.

And we finally get to see our first manatee. In need of air but not given to wasting energy, it rises slowly from the river bottom, on its back, flippers folded across its chest and its great upper lip in a sensuous pout. Fascinatingly, they have nostrils that roll open and shut, not unlike those pop-up headlights once favoured by sports car designers. Having acquired the oxygen it needs, it closes them again and returns slowly downward, head sinking first leaving its round belly briefly uppermost until lastly its large, broad tail disappears.

It is a day for visitors. During the afternoon, after a passage noticeable for its lack of other boats, we are approached by a small German sloop. It has a young man on the bow, waving energetically. 'Remember us?' he cries. We're sad to say we don't, but are concerned for his keel. We are already in very shallow water and his monohull will have a deeper draught than *Voyager*.

'La Gomera!' he shouts. 'Remember?' It obviously has some significance for him. I look hopelessly at David. His expression, as usual on these occasions, is blank. He doesn't remember faces. We first met at a jazz club and arranged to meet on the city centre's art gallery steps the following Friday evening. He had no memory of what I looked like, he told me much later, and simply got there early hoping I would recognize him.

The young man begins to explain but just then his wife calls from the helm to tell him that the water is becoming too shallow for them. As she reverses the boat and steers it away I see her for the first time, along with two small, fair-haired children. And then I remember.

It had been a bad, blustery, November night six months ago in the harbour of San Sebastian, the tiny capital of the small island of La Gomera in The Canary Islands. *Voyager* had been tied to the town quay at the time, with David reading in our saloon. But I had been unaccountably restless and had wandered up into the cockpit. Through the darkness and the beginnings of rain I had seen a solitary light bobbing towards the entrance of the dimly-lit and crowded harbour.

One of the nice things about sailing is the kindness of strangers. Sometimes it comes from coastal dwellers, who in language terms may share little more than a word or two but who instinctively know what you need. Sometimes it is the way fellow yachtsmen materialize and take your lines in what would otherwise be a difficult situation for a solitary crew member trying to cover too many urgent demands at once.

On that particular night, the little sloop lurching its way towards me through the buffeting wind and rain appeared to have only one person on board and with only a very tight space in front of our bows in which to tie up. I remember his look of relief to find someone there to take his lines. Only as I reached for his second one did I glimpse a young woman with two very small, fair-haired children clinging to her in the shadows.

Their boat would have taken a severe pounding that night, not just from bad weather but from the vicious acceleration zone surrounding the Canary Islands which creates sudden and violent increases in wind speed and sea turbulence. Perhaps that is why they remembered someone emerging out of the darkness to tie them up, combined with that overwhelming feeling of relief you get on finally reaching a safe harbour after a really bad passage. Their boat had gone when we rose next morning and I should never have recognized it again, nor its young skipper made anonymous by wet weather gear, rain and darkness. But he had remembered our boat.

6
A Night to Remember

We spend the night just north of Melbourne Bridge causeway with the anchorage all to ourselves. We wake to a glorious sunrise and another fine morning, which is just as well because twenty minutes after weighing anchor we run aground. We had set off through a maze of fishing buoys in the belief that we were in an open area of water with adequate depth, but were actually looking at the wrong page in the chart book.

Part of the reason is that the book is A4-size and contains 234 charts so you go through them fairly quickly and if you don't pay proper attention and keep turning the page you can suddenly look at the chart in front of you and not have a clue where you are.

Given the present debacle we decide that, since all the marker posts are numbered, every time we pass one we will write its number in the margin of the chart opposite its location, as a quick reference point. This will also serve as a discipline, to make us keep a check on the pages and where exactly we are, because it is very easy to let the mind drift off and simply gaze at the scenery. Like now.

The tide is on the ebb and it will be half an hour before it reaches its lowest point. After that we shall have to wait for it to rise again. So we have coffee and watch fishermen in small, shallow boats lift their fish traps - one fish to a trap and every trap has a fish in it, for this is a place of abundance. They are not the only fishers on the water this morning, however.

After helping build the nest, as soon as there are eggs in it, the male osprey takes on the job of feeding the female as well as himself and when they hatch, he shares the feeding of the chicks too. We now watch one of these dedicated parents hover over the water, not far from us.

The osprey is a raptor, catching its prey with its feet. When this one spots a fish he swoops. As he reaches it, his legs stretch forward and his wings go back. Seconds later he rises into the air with a very large fish in his claws. By its size it is undoubtedly very heavy compared to the bird's own weight so, to make its bulk less wind-resistant, once airborne the osprey moves one foot in front of the other, rotating the fish 90 degrees so that, like the bird itself, it is facing forward. This use of aerodynamics is something we'd read about but which, like the nesting osprey yesterday, we had never expected to see.

We also have the pleasure of being visited by three manatees, which glide contentedly by, grazing as they go, and a dolphin which doesn't loiter long, failing to find much of interest in a boat which fails to produce a bow wave for it to leap about in.

As we sit in the sunshine observing all this the young German from yesterday, a long way off in the distance, in the channel where we are supposed to be, calls us on the VHF to ask if we are in trouble and can he help us.

David says, 'Thank you, but there's nothing you can do. I've just been stupid.'

After a chat, and before signing off, as if still needing to somehow repay a perceived kindness in however small a way, the young man asks if we know about the rocket launch tonight. We don't. He's not sure of the exact time, he says, somewhere between 9 and 10pm he thinks but, 'Ask at the Addison Point Bridge.' And without knowing it, he provides us with what will become one of our most vivid memories.

Addison Point Bridge we discover, when we reach it 29 miles later, has two names. Its other one is the NASA Causeway Bridge at Cape Canaveral and the tender there turns out to be a mine of information. He confirms that there is indeed a launch this evening. It will be a Delta rocket carrying an unmanned satellite and the launch time will be 9.48pm precisely.

Although we had not intended to stop for several hours yet, we anchor mid-afternoon on the north side of the bridge in the shelter of its causeway, with the NASA building on one side of the river and the Astronaut Hall of Fame on the other. Ours is the only boat in the anchorage.

I have to make a confession here: I was never very interested in space exploration. I think it started too early in my development – teen years, rock and roll and all that. The planet I was living on was of far more interest than a barren moonscape and lots of scientists talking space technology. And orbiting satellites on the small television screens of the late '50s and early '60s never looked real somehow. But sitting waiting in your own cockpit, in the darkness of a warm Florida night, with the universe making itself felt all around you, is something else entirely.

The launch goes off exactly on time. There is a *huge* yellow glow on the bank opposite and the rocket roars up towards the stars. Then its great *boom* arrives, blazing pieces fall back to earth and a new satellite soars into orbit. The effect, as Americans would say, is *awesome*. Although not for the NASA workforce, apparently. From the bridge to our right has come a steady stream of car headlights since before the launch began. Their jobs are done. Routine now, after all these years, while home and hearth beckon.

As for David, he had been impressed by the US Air Force flypast at Fort Lauderdale, but this... well! And now the man who gave up acknowledging the anniversary of his birth at least a decade ago wants to know what else Florida will be doing for his Birthday *Week*. I ask him if he has anything particular in mind. He thinks for a minute and then says gnomically, 'Alligators.'

7
Location, Location

We wake to heavy mist just giving way to a hot sun, raise the anchor and make our way back into the ICW channel, but carefully since the anchorage is shallow and we do not want to repeat yesterday's ignominious grounding.

After that we just chug on, among the anglers and the birds - great solitary herons, flocks of egrets and pelicans – and, of course, the nesting osprey inhabiting the green markers down our starboard side.

For very soon you realize that there is a priority housing system at work here. Most desirable of all is the green marker post with a light on it, and for two very good reasons. Firstly, the small battery platform provides a secure base for the nest. Secondly being square, the two green metal marker plates turn the platform into a two-sided box for the nesting material as well as providing a perch for the doting parents to rest on while they tend their offspring; unlike the red, port-side triangles which are the wrong shape for perching on, and even when they have a battery platform do not hold a nest as securely. Mind you, one does wonder what effect these navigation lights have on these rather nervy birds as they flash continuously throughout the night. At least the parents can take it in turns to fly off and roost in a nice dark tree for a bit. The poor chick can't.

I suppose the most obvious question is: why don't they just build in trees? The answer, as always in the wild, is predators - eagles, large owls, racoons, anything that can fly or climb and has a taste for nestlings. Nests built over water, it seems, offer the best protection.

Next down the housing chain are the square green markers without a light. These provide a much smaller base – just the circumference of the wooden pile – but their two square sides do hold together the ramshackle type of nest favoured by the osprey.

Those piles with red triangles on but no platform are the least favoured and unless the female is particularly skilful, or determined, they are largely left unoccupied. Only in areas where there is most demand are they utilized and the poor parent can be seen teetering on top of an unstable heap of twigs that is very vulnerable to strong winds.

Having taken up a stance of non-intrusion in the osprey nesting programme, after passing dozens of plump chicks and doting parents I decide to risk just *one* picture for the album. We are approaching a large nest on a green channel marker. Inside it can be seen a big, yellow chick rhythmically raising its head towards a parent passing it food. As we get within range, I raise the camera very carefully and take aim. The camera refuses to take the shot and I try again, and again, but just as the shutter finally clicks the parent bird becomes unnerved and flies off, the chick ducks down into the nest and all I'm left with when the film is developed are some out-of-focus twigs. The only other form of wildlife we encounter today is one we'd rather have missed. Bugs.

Something a bit different though is the Florida East Coast Railway Bridge. While still a bascule, unlike all the others we have encountered it is not manned on site. According to the chart it is normally to be found open and displaying flashing green lights indicating that it is safe for water traffic to pass through; as, indeed, it now is.

On those occasions when a train is approaching, however, the green lights change to red and a siren blasts. If sensors below the bridge detect no vessels, the span lowers and locks into place ready for the train to cross over it.

It is an eerie moment. The waterway is deserted. There is no tender. Presumably there is a human being somewhere, in some remote spot, orchestrating events. But as you sail towards the opening you can't help wondering about what happens if the sensors fail and the bridge begins to lower onto your mast. Having had a bridge dropped on us in the Caribbean, this is not entirely neurotic imagining.

Or, what if an oncoming train has been given no warning that the bridge is open and cannot stop in time? The banks are heavily wooded so there is no way of seeing one coming. Would the trees and undergrowth muffle the sound of one arriving? Sometimes a few seconds take a long time.

Shortly after passing through we hear the bridge's siren, followed by the mournful sound of a distant train whistle. Of course. How stupid of us. Train drivers always sound a warning when approaching a potential hazard such as this.

A couple of miles further on, we leave the Indian River through a narrow strip of land via the Haulover Canal; inevitably where, by its name and before this small section of waterway was cut, people once had to haul their boats over dry land to enter the Mosquito Lagoon. And this is where the bugs we encountered earlier begin to multiply. In both senses of the word. Swarms of them. All of them mating vigorously. They land in vast numbers, all in a state of coitus and don't appear to separate, even for a minute.

They soon begin to drive me mad and David sends me below. After vigorously brushing myself free of them I shut myself in behind the insect screens and the companionway doors, turn on the computer and am well into the latest newsletter home when I hear David snap.

Out in the cockpit the carnage is terrible to behold. As is *Voyager's* wild-eyed skipper in the middle of it, still gripping a swatter. I take over the helm and send him below for a break. Never one to sit idly by, twenty minutes later he returns with sausage and egg sandwiches and two big mugs of tea. And thankfully, by this time, we have left the frantically mating insects behind.

The channel here runs close to the western edge of the lagoon. After about nine miles it becomes marshland, with hundreds of small islands, until finally we are surrounded by mangroves.

Eventually we reach the Ponce de León inlet, giving access between the ICW and the Atlantic Ocean. It is a name that resonates here in Florida particularly, and in America generally, thanks to the country's determination to outwit the aging process. Juan Ponce de León was a Spanish soldier and explorer who led the first European expedition to Florida and gave the state its name. Arriving off the coast here in April 1513 he named the land before him *La Florida*, because it was so verdant and because it was the Easter season, which the Spaniards called *Pascua Florida*, Festival of Flowers.

His own name is associated with the search for the fabled Fountain of Youth although not, apparently, until sometime after his death in 1521. Historians suggest that he was seeking gold rather than rejuvenating waters although nowadays, of course, they would be synonymous.

After the ocean inlet, the Mosquito Lagoon becomes the Halifax River where we anchor for the night in an area called Daytona Beach.

8
Daytona Beach

Our early youth coincided with the end of an era obsessed with land speed record attempts and the newspapers regularly featured the record-breaking activities of Britain's Donald Campbell and America's Craig Breedlove. Also, as a boy, David often visited the local Science Museum where the Railton Mobil Special driven by John Cobb, who had twice held the record, was a permanent exhibit.

Those particular record attempts were made on the Bonneville Salt Flats in Utah but, before Bonneville, drivers searching for somewhere long, straight and flat came here to Daytona Beach where the land speed record was broken five times between 1927 and 1935 – four of them by Britons: Henry Seagrave (twice); Donald Campbell's father, Malcolm (twice); and once by America's Ray Keech.

These earlier, Daytona Beach triumphs were so often referred to during the reporting of current land speed records – especially with both Campbell father and son driving a car called *Blue Bird* - that the name Daytona Beach became imbedded in our memories. So, having heard about it since childhood, next morning we decide to go and have a look at it.

It is a fair old walk down one of those very American roads that is wide and long, with no visible bus stops or passing taxis on it, and no pedestrians but us. My feet have become soft from going barefoot on the boat and I hadn't realized until now that my shoes still have traces of sand in them from our trip to the public telephone at Lake Worth. The effect is like having your feet gently but relentlessly sandpapered, but the visit is well worth the effort.

It is indeed a very long, straight beach with hard, flat sand and you know immediately you look at it and set your feet on it why they chose it. Its sheer length – travelling miles into the distance – gives it a strange quality. And standing with your back to the modern hotels and apartment buildings, looking out to sea, turning your head right and left and observing no perceptible curve to the coastline, you truly feel you are at land's end and that all there is - as there would have been for those racing pioneers - is a great howling emptiness.

The hardness of the sand is the other thing that forces itself on your notice. So hard that there are signs saying 'traffic lanes ahead' and '8mph max" because people are allowed to drive cars onto the beach for recreational purposes. It was even used as a general race track during the 1940s and '50s.

During the long walk back, and before returning to the boat, we stop off at the nearby supermarket for fresh bread. With the exception of a couple of shelf stackers the people inside are all pretty elderly, the customers especially. With my feet now feeling quite raw I have begun shuffling them, and as I move slowly around the aisles I become aware that the most elderly shoppers, some on walking frames, are nodding at me kindly as to one of their own.

After lunch we leave the very wide Halifax River, enter the narrow Halifax Creek and go along very nicely - passing some very attractive waterfront homes - until around 2pm. That's when *Voyager* slews toward the starboard bank and two small landing stages, each one with a speedboat hoisted up over it. Fortunately, rather than demolishing one or both, we come to a halt between them. Otherwise our detour would have been expensive.

The channel markers on this stretch of creek have long spaces in between them and clearly the dredged channel is even narrower along here than we thought. Once out of it, Voyager's keel had slid onto a shoal of mud which had then carried us smoothly but remorselessly, and at surprising speed, very close to the bank.

This is the third time we have gone aground in a very short space of time and highlights one of the few failings of our boat's design. Namely, that the transducer for the echo-sounder - which tells us what depth of water we are in - is located in our port hull. Since marine traffic laws require boats to keep to the starboard side of any waterway, we are able to run aground while our depth gauge is still showing plenty of water underneath our hull.

For a time we struggle to get off the mud, but fail dismally; just a great deal of noise and an embarrassing amount of smoke. One passing Jeremiah informs us that the tide here is a maximum of six inches and as he doesn't know what state of the tide we're in at the moment we could be in trouble.

Then the nice couple who own one of the little landing stages we didn't demolish come to see if there is anything they can do. We say, just put up with unexpected guests on your doorstep for a bit. They are busy replacing the deck in their back yard and suggest we could mow their lawn if we liked. David says thanks but he took up sailing to get away from gardening.

One of them goes indoors and checks the tide tables for us and says there is only a couple of inches left to go before high tide, which isn't going to be enough to float us off and back into the channel. They also tell us that this stretch is probably the narrowest part of the entire creek and that if you deviate just a smidgen from the channel you are onto the mud. We had shot from five knots in 10 feet of water to 2 feet and a dead stop in seconds.

The couple eventually go back to their deck-building and we wait for 'high' tide but still remain stuck. We have been here several hours now and are fed up. Then David spots two big sports fishing boats coming down the creek and radios them up to ask them if they would please roar past us. More familiar as these boat owners are to receiving abuse for their excessive speed and wash, they take a little convincing that he wants them to cause as much of both as possible when they get level with *Voyager*, but they finally agree.

They pass, one close behind the other, creating a substantial series of waves. Meanwhile David has both engines on full power and in forward drive. The waves from the two boats lift us just long enough and high enough to enable us to power our way off the mud bank and, for her first and only time, *Voyager* goes surfing.

9
St Augustine

At St Augustine we drop our hook south of the Bridge of Lions in a fairly crowded anchorage. It is also an unsettled one due to a 13-knot wind from the south and a one-and-a-half knot current from the north. This is causing us to be blown sideways, forwards and every which-way except to our anchor. The harbour is very attractive, however, offering even a severely-buffeted new arrival a delightful view of towers, a carillon and a bridge built in the medieval style.

According to our travel guide St Augustine was founded by the Spanish explorer, Pedro Menéndez de Avilés, in 1565 and is the oldest continuously-occupied European settlement in the US. Originally the territory had been tribal lands, before part of it was colonized by the French, who were then ousted by the Spanish who were in turn challenged for ownership of it by the English – not least in the person of Sir Francis Drake.

It was a turbulent period in Anglo-Spanish relations during which the two countries fought each other halfway round the globe. Among the better known encounters was Drake burning down Cadiz along with a lot of Spanish ships preparing for an English invasion (which Drake described as singeing the King of Spain's beard) and Catholic Spain sending a large armada to invade Protestant England with a view to replacing England's Protestant Queen Elizabeth with the Catholic Mary, Queen of Scots.

When the tide turns *Voyager* settles to her anchor and we head for the old town, stopping off at a tourist office for local information. The oldest house here dates from 1702 and the town belonged to Britain for a couple of decades from 1763 'after they swapped Havana for it' which sounds as casual as schoolboys trading in cigarette cards. Then ownership went back to Spain under the Treaty of Paris at the end of the Revolutionary War until the United States acquired Florida in 1821. The first slaves in America were brought to St Augustine the day it was founded by Menéndez, on September 8, 1565.

Inevitably the town has a strong Spanish influence in its buildings which, the booklet says, was maintained even in the building boom of the late 19th century. And in the last 20 years big efforts have been made to preserve its past. It is a very attractive, friendly town, full of large luxuriant trees, many of them in blossom.

It also has an impressive fort. Begun in 1672, the Castillo de San Marcos is the oldest masonry fort in continental America. We set off on a guided tour.

Popular American culture is one of moral certainties. In films and television good and evil are clearly defined, just as they were in the Westerns of my childhood where I recognised the good guys by their white hats and the bad guys by their black ones. This can also extend to popular history. It is taken personally. Them and us. So, at Castillo de San Marcos, instead of even the tiniest hint at the complex sweep of history as Europe's major powers - Spain, Portugal, England, The Netherlands and France – fought over the riches of the New World, the combatants at St Augustine are presented in the roles of good guys and bad guys.

Our official guide is a straight-backed, plump little body; her uniform straining across an ample frontage and a wide-brimmed hat at such a no-nonsense angle it would put a spirit level to shame. She asks the members of her group in turn where they are from. All are from various US States apart from two couples. The male half of the one beside us says, 'Germany.' Our guide nods approvingly and turns to us, still smiling. 'England', says David. Her smile evaporates.

From her features, fair hair and complexion – not to mention the north-western home State engraved on her name badge - it is a reasonable assumption that Gerda is not of Spanish origin so it is difficult to understand why she is taking it all so personally. However, I soon begin to take it personally as well.

David says I am being over-sensitive but, as I very reasonably point out to him, through gritted teeth, if she - and whoever wrote her script – had even an *inkling* of European history they might have known that this was not a matter of cuddly Spanish homesteaders trying to raise their corn and their children in peace despite the beastliness of Francis Drake. It was about spoils. Like other European adventurers flocking to the Americas, Spain's came looking for gold. Not finding any in Florida they sought it elsewhere

During the period currently under Gerda's scrutiny, a major source of plunder was South and Central America. It was loaded onto ships and taken to Spain. Their route took them up the Florida coast using the Gulf Stream to get them north, in order to pick up the Trade Winds that would carry them east across the Atlantic to Spain. St Augustine was strategically placed to provide their crews with shelter, rest, water and provisions. Not surprisingly it became a target for privateers like Drake. After all, why go to the effort of travelling all that way south to strip Inca temples or run gold and silver mines with slave labour, when you could simply hi-jack Spanish treasure ships as they sailed past your door?

But there is room for only one bad guy in Gerda's scenario. The English. As each date and attack is enumerated by our disgruntled guide, people in the group begin to turn and look in our direction. This is the first time we have encountered anything but courtesy. It is a shock.

'Why is someone so clearly of northern European descent bearing a 400-year-old grudge on behalf of the King of Spain?' I whisper to David.

'Dunno,' he says.

Gerda continues her roll call of dates and atrocities.

'No mention of the Spanish Armada turning up on *our* doorstep, then?' I hiss at him.

'Shh!' he hisses back.

But I'm getting really sick of the other people in the group scowling at us. Except the German couple who just look smug. And, thanks to a degree of shuffling on its part, what had begun as a group in front of the guide is still a group except for the two of us in isolation off its edge, like pariahs. So I devote my time to glaring at Gerda until we can move on to the next stage of the tour, a man's excellent and totally apolitical demonstration of flint lock musket loading and firing.

On the way back to the harbour we stop off at an old building which, once we get inside, appears to be dedicated to British brutality towards a Greek community said to have lived here later in the settlement's history. The first thing I see are whitewashed walls decorated with modern murals of gentle-faced Greek family members in heartrending poses of supplication in the process of either being starved or clubbed to death by the British. I've had enough American history for one day.

But a historical fall-guy is one thing. Live English visitors are quite another. Back in the anchorage our Red Ensign attracts a number of callers. A woman whose family came originally from London pops over in her dinghy; followed by someone about to set out single-handed for Puerto Rico, a passage we have recently navigated in reverse.

Our last caller is a man in camouflage shirt and pants who reminds me of someone in a movie that I can't quite place. After asking where we are from, and a brief chat about the area, our visitor turns his attention to the other people in the anchorage during which his demeanour changes. It seems he disapproves of a number of them but is particularly exercised by a man anchored near him who, he says, is making 'a *lot* of noise' working on his boat with power tools. And suddenly I recall the movie, a spoof in which a small band of excitable survivalists emerge from their desert retreat to deal with an environmental challenge threatening the imminent collapse of the social order.

The man in combat fatigues currently gripping our side rail says he has 'a high-powered rifle' on board and might have to 'sort the man out'. I assume he is joking but then decide he's not. Thin and intense, I can easily imagine him with a high-powered rifle in one hand and the thumb of the other hooked under bandoliers of ammo slung across his chest. David and I exchange a nervous glance and give our best impressions of two very quiet people on a very quiet boat.

Florida has another nickname, apart from *God's Waiting Room*. It is also called *The Orange State* because of the large amount of that particular fruit produced here. To flourish, the sweet orange requires abundant sunshine and water and the absence of frost, making Florida ideal.

Spanish explorers brought orange seeds with them in the 16th century because the value of citrus fruits in preventing scurvy had been long known in Europe, even though it would take until the early 20th century before the discovery of Vitamin C.

Scurvy - a nutritional deficiency resulting in suppurating wounds, jaundice, fever, depression, spongy gums, loss of teeth and ultimately death - could deplete a ship's crew on a long sea passage more comprehensively than either battle or bad weather.

In fact, it has been estimated that between the years 1500 and 1800 scurvy killed at least two million sailors. They were frequently at sea for long periods and the condition would develop after the fresh fruit and vegetables ran out. It was not uncommon for a ship to lose two-thirds of its complement to the disease.

The trees planted by these early Spanish explorers and colonists would form the rootstock and nucleus of future orchards throughout the Americas and the Caribbean. Some believe that Juan Ponce de León brought Florida's first orange seeds with him in 1513. Others date the introduction of the orange to 1565, when Menéndez founded St Augustine and where, two centuries later, one of the town's early entrepreneurs would begin mass production of the fruit.

10
Marshland and Swamp

We set off into a tranquil morning on the Tolomato River. It is flat and quiet out here; marshland with tall waving grass. Unfortunately, within a couple of hours of leaving the Bridge of Lions the tranquillity abandons us as we begin wielding our flyswatters like fencing masters.

Interestingly, Americans call these creatures 'greenfly', although any grazing British ladybird confronted by an aphid this size would tell you different. This American species has only its green head to justify its name because to all other intents and purposes it is a horsefly. And *very* determined.

Other insects tend to scatter when you flick a protesting hand at them. These simply duck and hang on, drawing blood. Their bite is painful and itches for days afterwards. Pity the poor horses. No wonder you sometimes see them thrashing and kicking and rolling on their backs. Our swatters hit the coaming and canvas awning with the sound of gunfire and soon we are jumpy and half deaf.

After a while the carnage on board *Voyager* ceases to be frantic and becomes rhythmic. Slap. Scoop. Slide the corpse down the cockpit grating. Slap, scoop, slide. And there is a tendency, when hit beyond a certain level of force – which does still occasionally reach the hysterical - for the green head to leave the body. Such is the determination of their assault, however, that the business end of one of our flyswatters splits and I end up below, feverishly sewing the two halves back together with carpet thread.

A yacht passes, the first vessel seen in hours. We had last encountered her in Antigua's Falmouth Harbour in February and renew our acquaintance with her skipper. Like us, they are under siege and their end of the VHF connection echoes with thrashing and banging and pain-filled cries of 'Arghh!' Fortunately, soon afterwards, the greenfly disappear as abruptly as they arrived.

Four hours into our journey we leave the marshes and enter the Cabbage Swamp. There are some small wooden dwellings along the river bank. They are the old-fashioned chalet and shack sort, redolent of get-away-from-it-all family weekends and men-only fishing trips.

Some distance further on, the river bank has been developed with waterfront houses, increasingly expensive the further north you travel, and all with private jetties. And soon you realize that there is an Interesting competitiveness at work here. What begins with a couple of pot plants on a simple wooden landing stage gradually becomes all about the size of your boathouse. One in particular resembles a Greek temple and is almost the size of one.

By mid-afternoon we have reached the St Johns River, a major waterway with large commercial ships sailing between the open sea and Jacksonville, Florida's most populous city and a major commercial and military deep-water port, 23 miles inland.

The crossing point is nearly a mile wide and very busy. After the narrow, sheltered creeks that we've been navigating for days now, it makes us feel rather exposed. Agoraphobic, in fact. So much so that we come to a halt at the edge of this enormous waterway and stare up and down it to make sure nothing is going to mow us down; which is ridiculous given that only ten days ago we were in the Bermuda Triangle dodging huge container ships.

We feel rather silly but very vulnerable, and most grateful when we reach Sisters Creek on the other side and can plunge back into marshland again. Perhaps the heat is getting to us. Our thermometer peaks at 99°F in the shade today.

Late afternoon we develop a wobble on the engine and David darts down to the fuel gauge. We have only a few gallons left. It never pays to go right to the bottom of a fuel tank for fear of contamination. So we turn back a mile or so, to an anchorage in the Fort George River just off the ICW, hoping there will be a service station nearby where we can fill a can.

A man in a small power boat pulls alongside for a chat and tells us there isn't anywhere here but where to find the nearest place tomorrow. We are glad of an excuse to stop early. It is barely 4pm but the heat today has been rather tiring.

The Fort George River runs parallel with, and only a short distance from, a beach although there is no direct access to the ocean just here. And despite being a recognised anchorage, it is a strange one in the sense that it is actually in the middle of the river rather than lying off one bank or the other. We currently have small boats, whose owners never bother about which side of a waterway they are supposed to travel on, rushing home from the beach down either side of us, sending *Voyager* bouncing like an apple in a water barrel. Such is the speed of their exit from their day of leisure I can't help feeling that if the three-minute warning ever sounds in the US this is what the country will look like to anybody standing in the way.

The evening cools very quickly and with the last power boat gone the river assumes a blissful quietness. Although not for long. Just after dinner rain arrives and it is soon torrential.

The river becomes uniformly flat and dimpled from the force of the rain while the countryside takes on a veiled, other-worldly look as if there might be nothing beyond the scattered trees except the same flat, grey landscape going on forever and ever. As the downpour gets progressively heavier, large areas of bank slowly disappear behind a curtain of mist and rain.

On the way here we passed some very attractive houses tucked away behind mature trees, but staring out of our windows now I feel I should not like to live in this kind of landscape. It has nothing to do with isolation – that is part of the allure of being a blue water cruiser - but with a creeping kind of desolation. It may have something to do with the way the water both nourishes and consumes marshland, making it appealing to the eye but at the same time dangerously inaccessible for anything beyond waterfowl and an occasional muskrat.

The summer storm, which had begun modestly with just a bit of heat lightning flashing behind some distant cloud, ends up directly overhead, with deafening thunder claps and lightning forking around us. We switch off all *Voyager*'s electrics to avoid a direct strike, our mast being the tallest object out here in the middle of the river.

Fortunately the lightning passes over by bedtime although not the rain, which wakes us sporadically, thudding down onto our decks and coach house roof and pinging off the metal air vents like grapeshot.

When we wake at dawn all the tumult has gone and the air has a crisp freshness to it. The dolorous effect of yesterday's rain has gone too and with sunrise the river takes on an ethereal beauty. Sky and water become pink and blue. A low, fine mist lies along the banks, and the trees stand with their feet in it like silent watchers in the pearly light.

11
Seeking Fuel

The ICW, when we turn back into it, is swollen from the night's rain as well as a high tide. The sun, as it climbs, turns everything to shimmering gold.

Our priority, however, is fuel. Had it not been, this is a marina we should never have attempted to enter. Its entrance is via a very narrow, shallow inlet which, by the time we reach it, currently has less than four feet of water on a falling tide. The fuel dock is at the far end of the marina in a tight dead-end. Its pontoon is only six inches above water level and, with the wind rising, it is a struggle to tie up.

This is a place intended for day boats and weekenders and having finally squeezed our way onto the fuel dock bow-on and tied up we stare hopefully about for someone to serve us. We try calling up on the VHF but get no answer so the only option is to throw myself off our very high bow onto the very low pontoon and go and find somebody. Every bone in my body feels jarred. The morning is already hot. The horseflies are out again and have been joined today by some enormous hornets.

After a search through tall, thick foliage I finally spot the small but deliciously air-conditioned office where the attendant is lurking and from where he must have had a prime view of my struggle to tie up to his fuel dock and get ashore. He is wearing a solar tope and does not seem excited about the prospect of following me outside. But as David says later, it never pays to expect a lot from a fifty-something wearing a solar tope and a pony tail. Although I think that type of knot in the nape of the neck is actually called a chignon.

We have just put the cap on the fuel tank, when a woman arrives asking with a sense of urgency if we need help getting off as she has three boats coming in. The implication is clear enough. They want us out of here.

We turn off the water, reverse out of the tiny fuel dock and set off for the channel leading back out into the ICW. As we enter the main part of the marina, the first of the three incoming boats is tying up and the second is approaching a pontoon. Suddenly aware of just how fast the water level is dropping, and keen to be out of here while there is still enough water for us to stay afloat, we are told to go back as the third boat coming down the channel has engine trouble. It is not yet visible and presumably the woman knew that when she hurried us off the fuel dock. The next 20 minutes are pure farce.

The man in the solar tope, his female associate and the couple from the first boat to arrive stand in a little group on a distant pontoon, watching. The man from the second boat hurries to where the disabled boat is slowly approaching. Because of the wind and the retreating tide, David has to hover in reverse in a narrow channel with moored boats on one side and a wall bristling with hull-lacerating barnacles on the other.

The attendant could have earned his keep by putting a dinghy in the water and pushing the ailing boat towards the pontoon or by grabbing a long rope and, as a man, been able to throw it further and so reached the poor woman on its deck currently desperately trying to throw her own ashore. Instead, he and his assistant stand as far away as possible simply following her feverish attempts with a look of concern.

Meanwhile, the solo sailor from the second boat strives valiantly to catch the woman's rope but it consistently falls short, and all her efforts and those of the poor man at the controls are in vain. In the process they hit a moored boat with a terrible crunch, and a wooden pile several times, and shunt back and forth until they are utterly miserable.

And still the thin man in the solar tope and his plump assistant stand there on the pontoon doing a passable impersonation of Laurel and Hardy. Meanwhile the tide is falling fast.

Finally, against all the odds the man from the second boat manages to catch the woman's rope and tie it to a cleat. By now David is beginning to look a little fraught with the effort of holding *Voyager* against wind and tide in such a confined space for so long and I ask the dynamic duo on the pontoon if we can please leave. We could pass with ease now and it will be much less trouble than having us blocking the middle of their marina when we run aground, which is going to happen any time soon.

The only useful person in the marina is currently trying to haul the stricken boat towards the pontoon against wind and tide but instead of going and helping him the man in the solar tope puts all his effort into waving us back towards the barnacle-encrusted wall and moored boats, all the time repeating slowly, loudly and distinctly, as if English were our second language,

'They ... have ... engine ... trouble.'

I am hot, sticky and bitten something rotten and I lose it completely. Like an infuriated Yosemite Sam, waving my arms in frustration, I yell back equally slowly, 'Yes ... I ... can ... see ... that,' and ask why the *hell* they don't try helping these people instead of standing as far away down the pontoon as they can get where they are of no use to anybody, least of all the poor devils on the disabled boat.

But the wind snatches my words away. It is up to 21 knots now and the couple on the boat are becoming desperate as it swings from its single mooring line. But as I'm yelling at the marina staff and pointing to where they should be, I see the worn-out woman on its deck looking at me miserably. Instead of being enraged at the marina staff for giving her no support, she thinks I am shouting at her and is crestfallen. It is not my finest hour.

David, meanwhile, has had enough. He puts our engines into forward gear and we drag our way out through the channel. By the time we reach the ICW the wind is gusting 28 knots and we are scraping the inlet bottom.

There is a strong current against us and the wind is on the nose so for a time we manage less than two knots. Our route today lies through Gunnison Cut - a canal through very small lakes - into Sawpit Creek, across Nassau Inlet, into the South Amelia River and on to Fernandina Beach.

On the approach to the latter we pass a small sand bar with dozens of dozing white pelicans. There are so many in a confined space that some are resting their heads and great beaks on one another's backs. This affability is one of the endearing things about pelicans. And like its brown cousin, it has the same quiet social habits.

Unlike the brown variety, however, the white one does not launch itself onto its dinner from a great height. It sits on the surface watching for a shoal, then sinks headfirst and pursues it underwater. There are two advantages to this. One is less damage to the bird's eyes than the brown pelican experiences from its plunge. The second is less likelihood of it colliding with detritus in the water that can cause serious injury, especially to that extraordinary beak.

The white pelican is comparatively rare and to encounter such a large flock of them, looking so pristine in the sunlight, is both a delight and a shock given the truly disgusting condition of the water here. There is also a terrible smell. The reason soon becomes apparent as we anchor between a power station and a chemical works. In the distance there are more chimney stacks pumping out more thick smoke.

Tonight I fall asleep with a white light flashing on a nearby chimney and the smell is worse than ever. We are caught in a wind over tide situation in a tidal river and take turns on anchor watch until 2am when the tide changes and *Voyager* is finally at rest.

Despite the fact that we are tired, and could do with a lazy day, we decide not to stay here another night. The stench is appalling. It is a depressing example of what industry – whose products we all use – can do to an environment. But in America, business is paramount.

An American will subsequently explain to us the national programme of credits allocated by government to a company in regard to some areas of pollution. Since 1995, he says, there has been a national system to curb sulphur dioxides and nitrogen dioxides to reduce acid rain. A plant is assessed as to what level of pollution it can reasonably be expected to produce and is then issued with emission permits or allowances. If emissions exceed the company's allowance, there will be financial sanctions. Conversely, and weirdly, if a company does not use its full quota, it can sell its remaining permits to another company which is about to exceed its own.

GEORGIA

12
Beautiful Places

Within half an hour of leaving Fernandina Beach we enter Cumberland Sound, a wide estuary surrounded by marshland, and fed by the usual assortment of rivers and tidal creeks. But, thanks to the wind, the estuary is pretty turbulent and with the Atlantic Ocean booming on our starboard side you could almost imagine you were out at sea again - an impression reinforced when we have to slow down to allow a submarine to cross our bows. It is not something we had expected to encounter in the notoriously shallow waters of the ICW and seems a little surreal.

When the sub has passed we curve to port, out of the Sound and back into the quieter waters of the channel and the shelter of Cumberland Island, the largest of Georgia's barrier islands. A barrier island is defined as a long, broad sandy island which lies parallel to a shore, has been built up by the action of sea and wind, and protects the shoreline. They will occur periodically all along our route and are essential in terms of giving protection from erosion to inland areas. Particularly as Georgia, along with South Carolina, is rarely higher than 20 feet above sea level and known for this reason as The Low Country.

Cumberland Island is around 18 miles long but with such a variety of ecosystems – maritime forest, salt marsh, mudflats, creeks, plus sixteen miles of sandy beach and sand dunes - that it has been declared a National Seashore which means it cannot disappear under waterfront development as so much of the eastern seaboard has. The island is home to deer, raccoons, armadillo, wild boar, alligators, mink and otter. Herds of wild horses graze its forests and marshland. Loggerhead turtles lay their eggs on its beach and sharks trawl the shallows.

On the opposite side of the river is the Kings Bay naval submarine base with lots of security zones bearing lots of signs forbidding you to approach. Having sailed in countries where you were warned not to even *look* at military establishments, and where to aim a camera at one meant immediate arrest, we try not to notice this one but it is so close you can't help it.

To the north of the main island, and cut off from it by marsh, is Little Cumberland Island which is not open to the public. There are wild horses on its beach; vibrant, glossy bays with long manes and tails. The horseflies seem more active than ever today and you really do feel sorry for horses, with such a large unprotected surface area available for biting and only their tails to use as swatters. Although some of them have the good sense to stand side-by-side facing in opposite directions, so that with each swish of the tail they not only brush their own hindquarters momentarily free of the wretched pests but their companion's face as well.

Today's journey takes us through a seemingly limitless marshland of waving grass and stunted trees criss-crossed by creeks and rivers. It goes on for mile after mile. The ICW is at its least developed through Georgia anyway, but here in particular you get an inkling of what the continent must once have looked like.

The birdlife, too, is wonderful. Wood stork. And our first-ever sighting of ibis. A flock of around thirty of them - wide white wings with black tips, long curved pink beak and long pink legs - fly over our foredeck. Arctic terns swoop into our wake for fish. They are dive-bombed by black-headed gulls, trying to steal their catch but too slow for the quick-witted and balletic terns.

Along the banks, Caspian terns trawl the shallows with open beaks. A cormorant on a marker post, very close and timid at the best of times, it wants to flee at our approach but has a large fish still only halfway down its throat. It cannot fly in this condition so has to stand there as we pass, frantically trying to gulp it down.

In St Simons Sound we follow the coast of Jekyll Island. There are people on its beach, salt water fishing, setting up long nets on poles. We have no idea how it works. It is not something we have ever seen before and we are past them and out of sight before we have time to find out. But it is as if a whole small community has come out on this sunny afternoon to work together: men, women and children all busy with their own particular task to do, and laughing happily as they work.

Across the Sound and into the Mackay River, we encounter *Holly Blossom*, a traditional American motor yacht of a type which is very comfortable for living aboard and travels at conservative speeds typically between five and eight knots.

It is known as a trawler yacht, which does become confusing if owners abbreviate it simply to 'a trawler' when using the VHF, leaving you staring around for a fishing boat.

The wife of the couple on board this one calls us up to tell us about one of their favourite anchorages, Fort Frederica, and even waits at the entrance to the Frederica River to make sure we find it as it is not part of the ICW. Nor is it somewhere we had thought to stop or even noticed on the chart. This sort of kindness and thoughtfulness, we will discover, is commonplace among Americans. They see your Red Ensign and immediately offer whatever hospitality they have available.

Nor is it limited to those afloat. Ask for directions ashore and the minute they hear your accent, they will strike up a conversation. Often there is a shared heritage or experience – British ancestors who emigrated here, military service in the UK, war brides brought home.

Before *Holly Blossom* signs off I take the opportunity to ask what the flock of large black birds wheeling languidly in the sky above us are. They are so *beautiful* in flight, gliding on the thermals with their wingtip feathers curving upwards in such a graceful way.

'Turkey vultures,' she says.

I look them up in our bird book and they truly are vulture by name and vulture by nature - and unbelievably ugly. Gazing up at them, circling remorselessly above your head, the thought strikes you: in such a can-do country as this one, do these creatures actually *wait* for things to die?

We have a little difficulty anchoring. There is a fast current here and a shale bottom. We end up swapping the CQR, which won't hold, for the Danforth and by the time we settle have come to rest some distance from *Holly Blossom*. Meanwhile, it is time for dinner and with one last look up at the black figures circling overhead I leave David to put on the snubbing line and head for the galley.

From the outset we had decided where possible to limit ourselves to an eight-hour day. This averages around forty miles which may not seem very much but given bridge openings, speed restrictions, negotiating mud banks and even the odd submarine it makes for quite a full day.

You are also steering constantly, unlike out at sea where we use the autopilot a lot. The channel is often narrow and it twists and turns so you need to concentrate to make sure you know exactly where you are on the chart. You are also endlessly changing from one waterway to another; need to know what to expect up ahead; be prepared to avoid vessels coming around bends from the opposite direction; and find a suitable anchorage at an appropriate time so as to be settled in before dark.

There will obviously be times when conditions, such as excessive heat or heavy rain, will make you want to shorten the distance, and others where the lack of a suitable anchorage requires that you extend it. And we are acutely aware of the time constraint on us. We need to be 35° North within the next eight days and an average of forty miles a day will get us there in good time. Today we have covered 42 miles and, given our late start, I knew we should not want to spend too much time preparing a meal. So during the journey I had set a big heavy pot of ratatouille going on the stove of all the fresh vegetables on board, plus tinned tomatoes and herbs, then sunk chicken fillets into it and turned off the heat. This way the meat cooks very slowly and you don't have to keep going below to check if it is burning to the bottom of the pan.

It is ready by the time we have anchored. Served with potatoes it is wonderfully flavoursome from the slow cooking. And the surplus ratatouille, now imbued with natural chicken stock and stored in the fridge, will make a tasty base for later meals or an instant home-made soup.

It is a tranquil evening filled with melodic birdsong and we sit in the cockpit after dinner watching a deep red sun sink down into the marshes. So very different an evening from our last two. Before going to bed David takes a look at the chart and notes that Fort Frederica, over on the eastern bank, is a national monument. Although out of sight behind the trees, it is only a short dinghy ride away. We decide to have a look at it in the morning after a much-needed, unbroken night's rest.

We are awake at four. Before going to bed we had gazed out over miles of tall waving grass. Now we stand on deck staring up at a long bank of mud in the moonlight, with only the roots of the grass visible and way above our heads. We have extreme difficulty orientating ourselves. Everything looks so different. We can't work out if we are even *close* to the place where we went to bed and *Holly Blossom*'s anchor light is nowhere to be seen.

Something long and large shoots upwards out of the water in front of our bows, snorting air through its blowhole before disappearing again and which for a moment startles us out of our wits. Unfortunately, it is not the only creature at large. The night is full of biting things, so small they bear the name 'no-see-ums'. But although you can't see-um you can most definitely feel-um. After establishing that we are not on the move, and that the boat is secure for a few hours, we decide to leave things as they are until daylight and bolt indoors again.

13
Fort Frederica

At around 7.30am we lower the dinghy and paddle off in a cool, fresh morning to a tiny wooden landing stage with an enormous tree drooping over it that could have come straight out of *Huckleberry Finn*. And thankfully the no-see-ums appear to be nocturnal and have gone. There is the most wonderful smell of mown grass coming from the site at this early hour and, as we walk towards it, the shafts of sunlight piercing the spaces between the towering trees make our entrance into Fort Frederica truly magical.

This fortified settlement was established in 1736 by General James Oglethorpe, as part of his defence of the fledgling British colony of Georgia. It became part of the wider battle being fought for domination of the New World, with the area being claimed by Britain, Spain and France even while Fort Frederica was being built.

At its peak the settlement was home to around a thousand souls and for a time seems to have thrived, not least on a generous diet of beef, port, game and seafood. The buildings were substantial: brick or tabby - a mixture of lime, sand, ash and oyster shells.

The Spanish made their only attack on the fort in 1742 but were defeated before they even reached it. Conversely, it was from here that General Oglethorpe launched his equally unsuccessful attack on the Spanish fort at St Augustine.

The site is beautifully kept and its information boards are a delight. We stand before the foundations of two terraced houses which, one such board informs us, were home to the Davidsons on the left who kept the tavern among other jobs, and Dr Hawkins the apothecary on the right. The Davidsons left the colony after a couple of years because of their next-door neighbours' intolerable behaviour.

Their flight is hardly surprising if the treatment received in the Hawkins' home by the visiting minister John Wesley, co-founder of the Methodist movement, is anything to go by.

Despite the travelling and privations involved in bringing spiritual succour to such an isolated settlement, the English preacher, theologian and abolitionist was threatened by the excitable Mrs Hawkins with a pair of scissors and then a pistol, being fortunate to escape with only the sleeve of his coat damaged – rent, we are told, by her teeth.

None of the tensions of living in a small, isolated community are evident now, of course. And we have the entire site to ourselves in the early morning sunlight.

After an hour spent wandering among the ruins of the fort, barracks, magazine, walls, moat and houses we paddle back to *Voyager* and leave the anchorage around 9am. The vacuum left by the no-see-ums when they clocked off at daybreak has been filled by horseflies. We rush through our anchor-raising so that we can take up a position in the cockpit where one of us steers and the other swats; reflecting that in what the world considers the ultimate throwaway society we may be the only people in the entire country to own a flyswatter with a darn in it.

The Frederica River is really only a loop off the Mackay River and we follow it north until we rejoin the Mackay and the ICW again. From there we enter the first of at least twenty different waterways with names like Buttermilk Sound, Little Mud River, Old Teakettle Creek, Bear River and the Ogeechee.

In our desperation to escape Frederica's insect population this morning we had failed to secure our anchor properly. A thoughtful Scots woman, married to a German living in Canada and taking a year's sabbatical on their yacht, calls us up to say it is dangling over *Voyager's* bow and swinging alarmingly. North America's boaters don't just contact foreign nationals with useful information, they exchange a bit of personal history as well.

Our anchorage for the night is just a left-hand turn and a short distance off the ICW into the romantically named Moon River. For who, above a certain age, can forget *Breakfast At Tiffany's* and that atmospheric theme song? Unlike the one in the lyrics, however, this stretch of water is not 'wider than a mile' but a modest creek. Its southern bank is formed by Burnside Island, which has houses built on it. The other bank is Pigeon Island and marshland.

We find a suitable depth of water to one side of the creek, allowing free passage for other vessels, and anchor behind the only other boat here. Its skipper, in a typically friendly gesture, comes out from his saloon, grins at us and shouts, 'Welcome to the neighbourhood!'

The neighbourhood is in fact a very expensive water frontage. And as dusk approaches the four children of the large house opposite leave their trampoline to play hide-and-seek through their landing stage, boathouse and substantial family runabout until summoned indoors to supper behind one of the house's many amber-lit windows. In contrast, a beam trawler returns from a day's fishing out at sea. The deckhands in their oilies wave to us as they pass. There is a most glorious sunset.

Around 1.30am David wakes me to say we have dragged our anchor. We can now virtually reach out and touch the reeds. It had been apparent when we entered the previous evening that the creek's bottom was very uneven, with sudden changes in depth, but we had finally anchored comfortably in eight feet.

In retrospect David thinks that what we anchored on may have been a soft mud 'shelf' and that when the wind changed, and the tide turned, *Voyager*'s anchor had been pulled off the mud shelf into water too deep for its length of chain. Although she had ultimately drifted back into the shallows, by the time the anchor had dug itself in again, we were almost into the bank.

We turn on the engines, lift the anchor and reset it further out. But, as *Voyager* swings around her anchor, the depth gauge oscillates between three and twenty-three feet. David stays up until 4am, by which time the tide has stopped running and we are lying normally in an appropriate depth.

14
Bonaventure

A couple of hours into our journey next morning we enter the Wilmington River. Two miles on, we pass a beautifully kept cemetery, high up on a bluff directly above us, with a lot of Stars and Stripes flying and a single Confederate flag. The site overlooks the tranquil scene we currently inhabit: a quiet river meandering between uninhabited islands.

Three miles from Savannah, and tranquillity itself now, the land this cemetery inhabits has a colourful past. In 1771 John Mullryne established a 600-acre plantation here which he called *Bonaventure*, as in 'successful enterprise' or 'good fortune'.

It also contained his country residence and small private cemetery both of which he beautified by planting *Quercus virginiana*, popularly known as southern live oak. Unlike Britain's deciduous variety, the live oak is evergreen and although it grows to only a relatively modest sixty feet, its width can be half as much again, the lower branches curving almost to the ground before sweeping back upwards.

In the American Revolutionary War (1775-1783) *Bonaventure* became a landing stage and campsite during the Siege of Savannah as Count Charles d'Estaing tried unsuccessfully to wrest the town from British control in 1779. The plantation house was turned into a hospital for French and Haitian troops and it is thought that some of the many casualties from these bloody assaults lie buried in the grounds in unmarked graves.

John Mullryne's fortunes waned after the war ended because he had supported Britain and King George. He was arrested and his property confiscated by the Georgia authorities for sale to the highest bidder. The family did redeem itself subsequently, and managed to buy the property back, but around Christmas 1803 the mansion burned down during a party and the land fell to disuse. For a venture named for success and good fortune it had been mired in bad luck.

However, the live oaks Mullryne had planted continued to thrive, their widely spreading branches host to the long, silvery skeins of Spanish moss that waft gracefully in even the lightest breeze. Over time, as other trees and shrubs, palmettos, ferns, wildflowers and grasses established themselves, the abandoned property gradually transformed itself into a serene place of ethereal beauty.

This was how the naturalist and writer John Muir discovered it in 1867, two years after the end of the Civil War. An advocate for the preservation of America's wilderness areas, he had set out from Indiana on foot for Florida. During his long walk south, and short of money, he rested for a few days at *Bonaventure*, sleeping at night on one of the tombs in the family cemetery.

Captivated by the sheer beauty around him – not least the magnificent live oaks - he wrote a chapter about it in his book, *A Thousand-Mile Walk to the Gulf*. This and his other writings would inspire millions of readers with their spiritual quality and enthusiasm for nature, not least the presidents and politicians whose legislation was essential in making America's national parks a reality. Muir himself was instrumental in the preservation of the Yosemite Valley and the Sequoia National Park, as well as the inspiration for many others.

Bonaventure would pass through several hands until purchased in 1907 by the City of Savannah as a public cemetery. One of those buried here is Johnny Mercer (1909-1976), who was born and lived in Savannah until he moved away to pursue a highly successful career in New York and Hollywood.

I sang along to his wonderful lyrics from early childhood: *Lazy Bones, You Smile and the Angels Sing, Autumn Leaves*. Songs filled with fun, romance or the echoing loneliness of lost love. He wrote the lyrics for more than 1,500 of them, won four Academy Awards and was co-founder of Capital Records.

Although his career took him away from Savannah, Johnny Mercer retained a home on the outskirts, his porch overlooking a tidal creek and the surrounding salt marsh. To honour him, following his death, the city renamed the creek – our anchorage of last night - after his Academy Award-winning song, *Moon River*.

SOUTH CAROLINA

15
Beaufort

The Savannah River forms the border between Georgia and South Carolina. As we cross it the crew of an enormous barge, on its way out to sea from the docks upriver, grin and wave. And I think that another characteristic I would add to my original list of 'big, rich and polite' is *cheerful*. Americans, whether on passing boats, behind store counters or driving buses seem invariably cheerful.

Our objective is the South Carolina town of Beaufort but we have already been travelling for seven hours, and are still three hours away. Also, towns can be difficult places in which to find a suitable spot to anchor late in the day, so we decide to find somewhere closer for the night. A couple of miles on we edge our way into a narrow backwater parallel with the ICW called Skull Creek and make our first real attempt at gunk holing.

The 'gunk' in the term refers to the typical muddy bottom of the coves and creeks, or 'holes', whose shallow depth and relative inaccessibility make them a magnet for the anti-social boater. This is because they are places where, even at the height of the sailing season, it is possible to escape the madding crowd and anchor in serene isolation with only birdsong and the lap of water to interrupt the silence.

We have arrived near low tide which is particularly useful because it enables us to see the limits of the space available for *Voyager*; in particular a sand bank which, had we unwittingly anchored with one keel over it and the other not, would have found us lying at a very lopsided angle in the early hours of the morning at the bottom of the next low tide.

As the only boat here we pick the most comfortable spot and with the evening drawing in, and the tide returning, much of the surrounding marsh gradually disappears and the houses on the east bank become water frontages again.

Sunset tonight is hidden by cloud, but later there is the most stunning moonrise - apricot-gold and more like a rising sun than the moon except that it sheds no light.

Once out of Skull Creek next morning we are briefly back in the May River before entering Port Royal Sound, a very broad estuary around four miles wide.

As every European yachtsman knows, marker buoys heading towards a port or harbour are green to starboard and red to port. In America the system is the reverse, but easily remembered by the mnemonic known as the three Rs: *Red Right Returning*. Accordingly, as we enter the Beaufort River the marker post colours change sides from green on our starboard side, as they had been in the May River, to red as we head for Beaufort.

We first encountered it last winter in the Caribbean, which also uses the American system of red right returning. And because it was so alien to us as British yachtsmen - and potentially disastrous in shallow or rocky waters if some markers were missing – that we became particularly alert to it.

So at first we are bewildered by the progress of the boat we now find ourselves following until we realize that its helmsman hasn't noticed that a change has taken place and is continuing to keep the green markers on his right hand side. In consequence he is weaving backwards and forwards across the channel into some quite dubious areas. Not to mention the looming disaster should anything large come suddenly around one of the river bends. David radios him up and the man settles on the intended route with relief.

It is always a pleasure to enter an old town from the water, but in Beaufort especially so. Spanish moss floats from the ancient and enormous live oaks lining the river. Side streets between magnolia-shaded houses remain unpaved, as they would have been when southern gen'lemen rode their well-groomed horses down them. Three-storey, plantation-style houses have their informal family porches discretely to the side, while formal two-storey porticoes, with classical Greek columns, grace their frontages. A white-painted wooden church with a very tall steeple glints in the sunlight. And you mentally shake your head to dislodge those early scenes from *Gone With The Wind*.

This first impression - that a time traveller from before the Civil War would probably feel quite at home here - turns out to be not too far from the truth. It seems the Union army occupied Beaufort as its headquarters and hospital zone for the duration of hostilities, thereby preventing the town from becoming a battleground and preserving it intact.

We go for a beer in the Old Bank Building and stay for a traditional southern lunch of crab chowder and shrimp sandwiches. Our waitress explains the difference between two towns with names spelt the same but pronounced differently. This South Carolina one is *Bewferd*, she tells us. The one in North Carolina is *Bohfort*.

With that settled we wander through the town's tree-lined streets and late spring blossoms, admire the lovely old buildings and stumble upon an old Episcopalian church where two British officers from the Revolutionary War lie buried.

About a mile and a half later, at the far end of town, we enter the wonderful Piggly Wiggly Supermarket. Its book keeper, doing her personal shopping in her lunch break and hearing our accents, volunteers the information that the checkout will call a cab for us when we are ready. Instead, the manager gets out his own pickup and drives us back to our dinghy. This is after they had already set us up a discount card so that we could benefit from their special offers, (including a new fly swatter) thereby saving us $5 on our shopping bill.

Back on board, with the other boats gone *Voyager* lies in glorious isolation. Just the barges passing en route to Ladies Island swing bridge some distance away. There is a ravishing sunset to accompany dinner, and another apricot-gold rising moon.

We breakfast next morning with a kingfisher perched on our pulpit, motionless, watching the water as he waits for his own breakfast to swim by. The American kingfisher is blue-grey with a large tufted head and twice the size of the British variety, although without its quicksilver flight and jewelled brightness.

We pass through Ladies Island Bridge just before seven into a glorious sunrise and a light south-westerly breeze. The bridge tender comes out from his office and leans over the parapet to wish us a very good day. It is hard to describe how pleasant the people operating these bridges are, or what a boost they give to the start of your day.

And today will need a boost. Today Aston Villa plays Chelsea in the FA Cup Final at Wembley. Chelsea is favoured to win so it could be a day of suffering for David.

16
Team Support

In sailing terms it is not an unusual day, in the sense that we pass from one river to another bearing the names of some of the many tribes and sub-tribes which lived along these waterways for thousands of years before the Europeans came. Rivers called Coosaw, Ashepoo, South Edisto and Wadmalaw.

The main difference is that, instead of running north and south as the ICW usually does, in the area north of Beaufort five meandering rivers run west to east, so that nearly half the time you are wandering along a river that is not going in the direction you want to go. Only when you arrive at one of the man-made canals linking them can you at last turn north for a bit, after which time you follow another river east or west until you reach another canal to take you north again.

Voyager's skipper, meanwhile, is enduring stress levels above and beyond those usually associated with fans whose team is about to take on the role of underdog in the traditional showpiece of the English football season. Adding to this tension today is BBC World Service.

It is bad enough that, just as you get used to your favourite programmes' times, somebody changes the schedules. An even bigger problem is that they also change the frequencies during the course of the day.

The reason given is that at certain times BBC programmes suffer increased interference. So it broadcasts on different frequencies at different times (none of which we know, not having access to its schedule) which means that having twiddled knobs for ages to find the programme you want, you are doomed to lose it without warning and have to mount a search to find it again. Ironically, when you do, the reception on the new frequency is likely to be worse than the one you've just had taken away from you.

Thus, after spending ages finding the right wavelength, at the moment the kick-off is due the programme disappears. A frantic trawl ensues. Once found, it is barely audible through the static and David spends the match out on the foredeck with earphones and a straw hat, sun blazing down and the heat tremendous, but the only place he can follow the commentary.

What is it about men and football? I confess I do not understand it. Football is one of the few things I do not share with David. Basically, because I do not wish to see this otherwise unfailingly cheerful, rational man in a state of anguish peppered with an occasional burst of blind rage. So during matches I usually arrange to be elsewhere. Today I am at the helm and he a furious, leaping figure on the foredeck – whether at the game or the radio reception I cannot tell and choose not to know. Aston Villa lose 1-0. I knew they'd let him down. After an initial moment of disappointment, however, he takes it philosophically. David takes most things philosophically.

Although the distance covered today has been 36 miles, we have probably travelled only twenty in the direction we want to go. Early afternoon, after a short distance on the Wadmalaw River, we follow *Skipper Bob*'s advice and head up the narrow inlet of Tom Point Creek, 'continue a mile and a half upstream for wind protection from the trees on either side' and anchor in blessed isolation for a lazy afternoon away from the Saturday crowds.

Sunday brings out the speedsters. And the rich at leisure. The really big stuff comes out on Sundays. In a very narrow part of the channel an enormous motor yacht surges past, slices in front of us and then lurches almost to a halt.

Thrown forward against our windscreen as we are, we peer up into its impressive bridge and wonder if they even saw us, so absorbed are they; standing looking down at a chart, like a tableau almost. Posing at each other. Two males and a female, all three in their white summer plumage: the former in what look like linen suits; the latter in a wafting sort of fabric and one of those 1930s-style cloche hats. Then they roar off, leaving us bouncing in their wash.

17
Charleston

We try to anchor in Charleston Harbour but all the most suitable spaces are filled. Unable to find a reasonable depth, we abandon the anchorage and call up the marina instead but the instructions confound us and we get into a right mess, largely because we go *inside* 'the outside wall by the fixed flagpole' when we should have gone 'outside and tied up on the inside'. We find it a confusing marina altogether, as if it began small but then developed outwards in a not-altogether logical form, making directions over a VHF difficult to follow. We find the right pontoon ultimately, tie up beside a trimaran and have a seafood dinner nearby. The town is noted for its restaurants.

Charleston is the oldest and second-largest city in South Carolina. In 1663 King Charles II granted the chartered Province of Carolina to eight of his friends although it took a further seven years for the first of the expeditions to get going. In 1670 it founded Charles Towne which meant the king got his name in twice: as both the settlement's name and that of the province, Carolina being derived from the Latin *Carolus*, meaning 'Charles'.

This early settlement was subject to assaults by the Spanish and French (both of whose sovereigns were eager to settle the region for themselves), by pirates and by local tribes resisting any further expansion into their lands. In 1783, following independence, its name was changed to Charleston – sometimes referred to as Chuck Town.

We are woken around 2am by blue flashing lights and loud voices. Several police launches are patrolling up and down and someone is shining a torch into unoccupied boats. There's rarely much peace in a big marina but their facilities are always welcome. We are up at 6.30 and give *Voyager*, ourselves and our laundry a thorough going over, before setting off into Charleston.

When we reach the bus stop we find we've forgotten the DASH bus map - given to us by the marina when we registered. We end up getting on the wrong vehicle, but the delightful driver sells us a $2 all-day ticket each and puts us on the right one. It takes us up a broad avenue lined with lovely old houses and very obligingly drops us off right outside the post office. I am reminded of that old chestnut about the elderly London toff, berated as elitist and out of touch with the real world, who sets out to prove his detractors wrong by climbing onto the first bus to come along and saying imperiously to the driver, 'Eaton Square, my man, and quick about it.'

There are four envelopes of mail waiting for us at the post office, including birthday cards for both of us. We have cheese Danish and coffee in a lovely old wood-panelled bar with a beautiful ornate ceiling, and a quick read through our letters for anything that needs answering. There isn't, so we seal up our newsletters and go back to the post office with them, taking the time to wander around its little museum.

After that we take a meander through the town's 18th century buildings, from stately, multi-storey mansions to small cottages, cobbled side streets, horse-drawn (and even ass-drawn) carriages and historic churches - two apparently claiming to have the same two City Fathers buried there, but maybe we went round in a circle. That's the nice thing about meandering. You don't worry overmuch about dates and names. The mind simply enjoys the ambience, the shapes and colours and textures, the luxuriance of the trees and window boxes, and the sheer courtesy and helpfulness of the people.

At the bookshop near the university I buy a copy of Virginia Woolf's *To The Lighthouse* because I've always intended to read it, plus *The Scarlet Letter* and *The House Of The Seven Gables*, both by Nathaniel Hawthorne because he's an esteemed American writer and we're slowly heading towards the New England territory about which he was writing.

We get a DASH bus back to the marina and are just getting *Voyager* ready to shove off when our neighbour from the trimaran returns carrying a large takeaway coffee. A friendly man, and a cruiser like us, he asks us where we are planning to spend the winter. We tell him we haven't decided yet.

The Bahamas, he says. Safe, friendly and, apart from the likes of Nassau and Freetown uncrowded, because most of the people who go there are cautious and stick together, leaving large areas untouched. 'Seven hundred islands,' he adds. 'And most of them uninhabited.'

I think we know where we're going for the winter.

When you leave the marina to head north you sail a short distance down the Ashley River, with its historic waterfront of lovely old buildings and shady gardens. But quite soon the waterway opens out into the lower reaches of Charleston's very wide harbour where several rivers converge.

Then in no time at all you find yourself approaching the harbour's most distinctive feature: Fort Sumter, famous in the annals of US history as the place where the American Civil War started.

On December 20, 1860, only six weeks after Abraham Lincoln's election as President, the South Carolina General Assembly voted to secede from the Union. A month later, cadets from Charleston's military academy fired on a Union ship entering the harbour. Then on April 12, 1861, General Pierre Beauregard ordered the shore batteries to open fire on Union-held Fort Sumter. After a bombardment lasting 34 hours the fort surrendered and the Civil War had begun.

In retaliation, Union forces shelled the streets of Charleston with two-hundred pounders and blockaded its harbour to commercial traffic. It was during the Confederate's attempt to destroy the blockading Union ships that one of the earliest military submarines went into action. It was called the *H.L. Hunley*, after its inventor. At a little under 40 feet, and with a propeller cranked by hand, it sank the 1,124 metric ton USS *Housatonic* in a night attack on February 17, 1864 but failed to return to its base.

Five of the warship's crew lost their lives that night but overall the sub itself lost many more. Including the attack, plus two earlier sinkings during training, the *Hunley* caused the deaths of 21 of its own crewmen including Horace Hunley himself. The submarine was eventually found in 1995, under several feet of silt which had both hidden and preserved it for 130 years.

Criticised at the time, for the large loss of life among its own mariners during its six month career, the *Hunley* made history as the first combat submarine to sink an enemy ship in undersea warfare. Plans are currently underway to raise it.

As we are quite late leaving Charleston we plan only a short journey before tucking ourselves into one of the many creeks running off either side of the ICW for the night.

It is a cool overcast afternoon threatening rain that never comes. Local beam trawlers pass, on their way down to Charleston Harbour and out to sea for a night's fishing. With their nets out over their beams like translucent wings, they look for all the world like giant mosquitoes, especially on a grey, hazy afternoon.

18
Barefoot Landing

It is hot back out on the ICW next morning, despite the early hour. On one of the jetties a cormorant perches on a wooden pile and stretches its neck. A pelican dozes on another. On a strip of timber at the back, a line of laughing gulls shoot the breeze, while the landing stage itself is littered with small sandpipers.

In the midst of them all is a large brown owl. Not a real one but a type of plastic bird-scarer of which people here make prodigious use. They fasten them everywhere – on their boats' pushpits and awnings and even on occasions at the top of their masts. On shore they put them on lawns and landing stages and over goldfish ponds.

Real birds, even the smallest, either treat these 'owls' with indifference or adopt them as one of their own; so that even when there is plenty of room to roost well away from one, small groups will gather around it as if it provides a focus for their repose.

Today's passage is mostly on man-made canals rather than rivers or lakes. American canals are different from the British ones we've sailed on. The latter's sides are usually lined with brick, stone or concrete and supported by strong banks and a tow path. The ones we are on now are trenches dug from the soil, flooded and susceptible to erosion.

At one point David thinks he can see a red-and-white lighthouse through the trees, which is odd because we aren't within sight of the coast. It turns out to be a very wide red-and-white striped tug and barge which inevitably we pass on one of the narrowest stretches of channel.

In the meantime, things are very frustrating on the photography front. My beloved instamatic is no more, succumbing finally to the effects of salt air, and the big camera won't speak to me. Every time I try to focus it, it takes an out-of-focus photograph instead. On the rare occasion that it agrees to focus, the shutter release doesn't work. And failing all else I've usually got the wrong size lens on it when something wondrous happens.

We anchor for the night in a stretch of water behind Butler Island, lake-like and deserted except for us. There is a rumble of tugs from the ICW throughout the night but it is not at all intrusive, just a little eerie as they pass unseen on the other side of the island.

Next morning David finally has his first alligator sighting. Early in our journey we had ruminated on why we never saw any sailing schools in all this abundant, sheltered water. The first time you see a pair of large, hooded eyes gliding on the surface you know why. Mind you, it could really put some zip into the average capsize drill.

We also spot our first mile marker - 385 - in a cypress swamp. We've been looking for one since Fort Lauderdale. It means we are 385 miles from Norfolk which is the official start of the ICW except that we started from the other end. We pass some abandoned rice fields.

In places there is a shortage of channel markers for the osprey to build on, so some of them are forced to build in trees. I spot a male carrying a large fish up to one of them. It forms a graceful silhouette against the sky, but the camera takes the shot while I am still trying to focus and by the time I take another the bird is lost against a background of trees.

The ones along here grow right to the water's edge. At high tide the water rises above their roots but leaves them high and dry at low water. The banks are dense and dark and initially rather oppressive but there are pale dots among the dark trees. After peering through the binoculars the answer finally emerges – the native swamp rose. Pink and five-petalled. There is also a heavenly perfume that is most un-swamp-like. It is honeysuckle and for miles and miles the waterway smells like an English summer hedgerow.

Small turtles walk along fallen tree trunks or doze on them in pairs. And we see our first bluebirds. It confused my childhood no end, having Vera Lynn singing about them flying over the White Cliffs of Dover because England didn't have any, except on Bluebird Toffee tins. It was only decades later that I discovered the songwriters were American and so are bluebirds, only nothing like the ones on the toffee tins.

There are also huge butterflies fluttering across our decks. What with them, and the bluebirds overhead, and tiny turtles and wild roses on the banks it's a bit like falling into a scene from a Disney animation.

And this might be the place to mention those who have made our journey possible because since 1824 the United States Army Corps of Engineers has had responsibility for the ICW's improvements and maintenance. Unfortunately, or so we have been told, successive governments have cut back their budget so that the waterway is years behind on maintenance. The reduction in dredging has meant the water becoming ever shallower.

We have already negotiated a number of such stretches but the problem is particularly apparent now as we approach a place called Barefoot Landing. Here it is very obvious that the banks have been considerably eroded, most likely by the wash from boats. As the banks have been undermined, and the mud has sunk to the bottom, the waterway has become wider but increasingly shallow.

On all the charts, and in a lot of areas, there are No Wake warnings and reminders that *you* are responsible for *your* wake. But a large percentage of boaters ignore this and there seems to be no-one enforcing the rules. Ironically the boats most capable of making excessive wash tend to have a shallow draught and are therefore unaffected by the silting up.

As if to emphasize the problem, as we approach Barefoot Landing we have to ease our way around a grounded tug and barge. The vessel's captain looks most unhappy.

We tie up at Barefoot Landing, just managing to get onto the end of the floating dock without touching the bottom. It is a new development and not on the chart yet but it is in *Skipper Bob* and you can stay here free for 72 hours.

Nearby Myrtle Beach is a holiday resort and Barefoot Landing is a factory outlet mall full of brand name shops but no food store. So David sets off for the Harris Teeter supermarket, which the mall's security guards tell him is only half a mile away. It is more like two, and a very hot day. In the US distances are inevitably underestimated because everybody has a car. Inevitably, places are perceived as closer than they really are and most often described to you as: *About half a mile down the road*.

While he is away an American couple from an English catamaran, a Heavenly Twins called *New Horizons*, come and introduce themselves. They are currently ferrying an elderly folk boat – a small traditional European yacht - up to Chesapeake for the owner along with his elderly spaniel. A good-natured, cheerful soul, she wanders like a canine Pollyanna through a loving world completely oblivious of the fact that to other denizens of this place she is considered food-to-go.

Among the attractions at Barefoot Landing is a cage of tigers, who take a great interest in her as she trots innocently down the boardwalk with her minders. And on the way here, apparently, after catching sight of her on board the boat an alligator had taken to cruising alongside for quite some distance. Not long after telling me this, both of them absent-mindedly leave the boat unattended for a short time and the dog goes off to look for them. So it is not surprising that they succumb to a panic attack when they return and find her gone. Happily all three are soon reunited.

David is gone so long I decide to go up into the mall and buy a take-away pizza so that there will be some sort of meal ready when he gets back from the supermarket. I buy the smallest available but it's surprising how big an 18-inch pizza is. Something you learn very quickly here is that where food is concerned there is no such thing as 'small'. Still, that's tomorrow's lunch taken care of as well, leaving more time to look around.

There is a lake here, with graceful snowy-white egrets and terrapins, and the caged tigers, of course, and a great many shops. The most surprising to us, is a large one selling nothing but Christmas decorations. In fact, over time it will become quite usual to encounter an all-year-round Christmas decorations shop. How they make a living is beyond me. But then, how so many shops in so many shopping malls the length of the country with virtually nobody in them most of the time make a profit seems to defy logic.

In the meantime, it's Motorbike Weekend at Myrtle Beach so along with buckets and spades, fishing poles and shrimp nets you can buy a T-shirt with, *If you can read this, the bitch fell off,* printed on the back.

At Sunset Beach, 17 miles north of Barefoot Landing, we reach a pontoon bridge, a type we have not encountered before, nor are we likely to anywhere else as it is the last of its kind still in use on the east coast. Dating from 1958, this wooden, single-lane bridge has a cream, two-storey tender's hut - like a small clapboard house with striped awnings at its upper windows - on its middle section which is also the floating pontoon.

When boats need to go through the bridge, this pontoon is pulled away on cables, after which the boats have to wait for the cables to sink to the river bed before it is safe to pass over them. We are one of 15 boats, backing up and circling, during the quarter of an hour wait for the bridge to open. *New Horizons* and the little folk boat they are ferrying north just make it in time to get through. The folk boat cannot manage more than four knots but the spaniel prefers a gentle pace anyway.

NORTH CAROLINA

19
Carolina Beach to Mile Hammock Bay

We enter North Carolina mid-morning. There is a dead alligator lying on its back on the starboard shore, with its short legs in the air as if it has died in the water and been washed up onto the mud. It is the only complete alligator we shall ever see. The rest of the time it is just two hooded eyes on the water's surface.

Much of today's journey is on canal but the waterway becomes very broad as we enter the Cape Fear River. Like Florida's Indian River it is extremely shallow with a narrow, navigable channel dredged through it. Most of the other boats stop here. We continue on to Carolina Beach Basin, ten miles further up the river and through a short, deep-cut canal with high banks.

The Carolina Beach anchorage is a small bay at the north end of Pleasure Island. It has waterfront villas, each with its own landing stage at the bottom of the garden. All have modest-sized leisure boats on them except one, which has a large commercial fishing trawler parked on it. The marine equivalent, I suppose, of taking the company vehicle home for the weekend.

The Basin is a well-protected spot with a handful of tiny islands dotted about in it. It also has good holding, a reasonable depth and is only a short distance from the ocean which is currently providing a refreshing sea breeze. Today's journey has been just over fifty miles and very hot. The evening produces a violent thunder storm followed by very heavy rain. This is a nice little place to be tucked up in on a turbulent night.

As we leave next morning the rising sun makes a brave attempt to unveil its glory but is trapped behind the houses lining the bank between the basin and the ocean. It manages briefly to turn a narrow stretch of water scarlet but anything more dramatic is thwarted by heavy cloud.

Before it disappears completely, however, its brief glow makes a little jumble of wooden buildings and higgledy-piggledy jetties look even prettier than they had before, with a pelican on every pile, airing their wings like so many church lecterns. For some people natural shapes do not quite foot the bill as garden furniture, however, and we pass a huge silver fairy on somebody's lawn, complete with magic wand. Three doors down there is a life-size giraffe, its head at roof level.

Our journey continues parallel to the coast, about a mile from the sea, through marshland and small islands. At Wrightsville Beach Bridge two men on jet skis slink past, suspicious-eyed. One heavily built and dour in shades of khaki, the other younger but solemn in a grey shirt and navy blue body protector - the local sheriff and his deputy.

In places enormous multi-level houses, their roofs over-run with dormer windows, have been built on the marshes. Though technically waterfront homes, they are some distance from the water to take advantage of solid ground. This requires very long jetties to reach water deep enough to float their boats. One of the jetties, undulating with the contours of the marshland, is so long it has a bicycle shed at both ends.

And there are lots of nesting osprey. One of the nests I look into has three fluffy yellow chicks, quite large ones, sitting in a row. At another the male is just flying away towards the bank with what looks like the remains of a meal while the female tidies up the rear end of their offspring.

We stop for fuel; the cheapest we will encounter at 59 cents a US gallon, or 10 pence a litre. As we prepare to leave, the man on the wharf untying us observes David at the helm, his back toward us, and makes a quip about leaving him here and himself coming along with me instead. He has a nice face, but sad. I say I wasn't planning to make a change, but if I do, I'll get in touch. 'Does he never shout at you, then?' he asks. 'David?' I say. 'Heavens, no!' As he frees the last rope and hands it to me he says his own wife left him early. 'Colon cancer. Else we'd be doing the same as you.'

We anchor for the night in Mile Hammock Bay, in a basin dredged by the US military training facility of Camp Lejeune, a 246 square mile Marine Corps base camp. You are not allowed to land here but are welcome to anchor in this sheltered and calm little bay. A family from the camp fishes from a wooden dock.

Skipper Bob recommends that you let the anchor sink into the silt here for a while before you pull back on it to set it. Accordingly, people loiter at their bows, waiting, sociable in a glorious sunset that morphs from gold to flame to deepest red.

Next morning a few boats set off for the 7.30 opening of Onslow Beach Bridge and we become part of a small flotilla. The waterway now takes us between the coast and the massive Camp Lejeune base. About four miles from the anchorage, the bridge marks the start of the camp's firing range.

If the range is in use, this bridge and section of the ICW can be closed for hours. Fortunately nobody is firing at present. There's just smouldering trees in the distance and the faint smell of wood smoke.

In one place a dredger is lying right across the channel. A large trawler yacht runs aground trying to get round it. And while there are several inviting little inlets and bays in this vicinity the chart warns of 'unexploded projectiles' so it's best not to stray.

At Swansboro we get into frenetic small boat traffic which becomes steadily worse so that by the time we reach Morehead City it has become bedlam. 'I know it's Saturday,' someone grumbles over the VHF, 'but Jeez...' Somebody else reminds him that it is also the start of Memorial Day Weekend.

Memorial Day takes place every year on the last Monday of May in memory of the men and women who have died while serving in the US Armed Forces. As in Britain, America's national holidays occur on Mondays and the previous weekend is joined to it, making today the first day of the three-day Memorial Day Weekend. It also marks the start of the summer vacation season which explains the unusual amount of vessels afloat today.

The waterway is also very wide here, and choppy. We are surprised to see small, two-man Wildlife Patrol boats stopping leisure craft to request a reduction in their speed. It is the only time we will ever see any attempt at speed control.

We reach Beaufort. This is the North Carolina one pronounced *Bohfort*, and not to be confused with the South Carolina one which prefers *Bewferd*. The water traffic here is so dense that we decide not to stop but continue on to Cedar Creek, a spacious bay just off the ICW.

20
Cedar Creek

From Cedar Creek there are only four miles to go to comply with our insurance requirement to remove ourselves from the Hurricane Zone by the first day of June. So we can afford to take Sunday off.

By mid-afternoon the anchorage has started to fill up - around a dozen boats – with the lightest of winds coming from the south although the sky to the north has become dark and rather menacing. We continue facing south into a light, warm breeze, but as a precaution I take our laundry indoors and all the loose items lying about on deck. The clouds behind us turn black and move closer.

Around 3pm a squall hits from the north and spins us through 180 degrees. Our anchor breaks loose but resets itself very quickly so we are no threat to other boats. Horizontal rain lashes us, visibility is negligible and the wind speed indicator registers 35 knots or Gale Force 8.

Meanwhile our neighbours do some dragging of their own, three of them a little close for comfort. *Apotheosis*, a 45ft ketch, passes within a few feet of our bow but with no-one on deck. A 30ft sloop hobby-horses like mad as it canters down our port side, while a small trawler yacht glides rapidly along our starboard beam.

A difference between European and American yachtsmen is that the former use chain to attach their anchor while Americans favour rope. The latter is cheaper and easier to lift, but there is less snatch with chain and its sheer weight helps the anchor to grip.

Another advantage of chain is that it can alert you to the fact that you are dragging. If you are below, and unaware that you are on the move, the chain's vibration on the bow roller will be audible through your hull. And, as has happened to us here and at several other places recently – at Fort Frederica and Moon River in particular - within a very short time the anchor will reset itself. This is why the people dragging around us on rope are unaware for longer and travel further.

The other boats are soon re-anchored, however, apart from *Apotheosis.* Having finished up on the shallow southern bank, it takes a fair bit of effort to extricate it from the mud.

It is tranquil by bedtime but around 1am the wind gets up and it starts to rain again, so I go and make sure all the hatches are closed. David goes to check that we are still in the same position as when we went to bed and notices that *Apotheosis* is on the move once more, bumping into other boats and heading for the southern shore again. But, having failed to achieve yesterday afternoon's ferocity, the wind finally settles and we return to bed.

Monday's 6.30am weather forecast says to expect 25- to 30-knot winds. It is also surprisingly cold, and raining. So we make breakfast and take it back to bed, opting for another leisurely day. We can afford a second day off. But the present erratic weather is a reminder of the dangers in cutting a journey's time too fine and having to travel in poor conditions.

It may be cold and wet outside, but it is snug indoors. Fisherman's socks for me while David unearths his old carpet slippers. The only thing missing is a log fire. The anchorage is now deserted except for us, so everything is nice and relaxed until after dinner when a very large trawler yacht called *Calypso*, registered in New Jersey, arrives. It has two twenty-somethings on board, one in a baseball cap the other with floppy hair. They drop an anchor off our port bow, let out too little rope and drag. They retrieve their anchor, sidle across in front of us and drop it off our starboard bow, again with very little scope.

They are too close. It will be touch and go if, when we both swing, we will miss each other. We sigh and are about to return to Trollope's *Barchester Towers* when they toss a second anchor over the stern. Now there is no question about it. With *Calypso* held in place by two anchors, and us swinging into the wind on one, a collision is inevitable. We look across at the two young men. The one with the floppy hair waves in a patronizing sort of way. David starts to explain the problem but both men turn away, go below and switch on their television.

By anchoring as they have, in an otherwise empty bay, they are effectively saying, 'If you don't like it, you can move.' David tries to reach them on their VHF but it is not switched on – or they choose not to answer.

It is not long until nightfall. I had been anticipating a restful evening and a gentle decline towards untroubled sleep, given the lack of wind or other boats. Although after yesterday's unexpected squall we cannot depend on the present lull to continue.

We have a choice. We can either move, or put out a stern anchor ourselves. The problem with the latter is that, as we have already discovered, with Cedar Creek's soft mud bottom some dragging is almost inevitable in a strong wind. And two anchors dragging can get into an awful tangle. We sigh again and go below to exchange our present casual footwear for deck shoes and prepare to move.

Insurance is the crucial factor. In the event of serious damage, how do we prove we were here first and that they anchored irresponsibly? It becomes our word against theirs. And anyway, it would take up too much time. Our summer idyll has barely begun. We don't want it mired in argument and insurance claims.

By the time we return on deck, however, a wind has risen. Fairly light, but enough to establish without question that *Calypso*'s two anchors - the one off the bow with too little scope, and the one dropped as casually as a fender over the stern - are simply weighing her down on the spot rather than anchoring her to the bottom.

As the wind strengthens, the trawler yacht begins to drift. Fortunately she misses our bow as she sets off towards the same muddy bank and shallow water for which *Apotheosis* had shown such a marked attraction yesterday; only a bit further over to the right, where the shoreline is littered with fishing buoys.

We don't bother trying to raise them on the VHF as they are not answering it anyway. And they wouldn't be able to hear us shout to them over their television either. David returns to his slippers. I stay in the cockpit, keeping a weather eye open.

After a while there is much activity on board *Calypso*. A lot of running about to start with. Then an engine fires up, after which two figures are bent double over the stern for some time, pulling - as far as I can make out through the binoculars - at what looks like rope in the general area of their propeller. It might be from their stern anchor; or maybe one of the many fishing buoys in that area. And I'm not sure, when they finally come to rest, if they are still afloat or not. If they are, they are lying at a very odd angle to the wind. Anyway, there they stay.

The forecast next morning is still not brilliant, but better, and we do need to make a move. Not just to be above 35° North but because our food supply is no longer the enjoyable mix and match it once was. Basically, while we will not go hungry for a while yet, the possible combinations will become less tempting by the day.

21
Oriental

We leave Cedar Creek in a cold, damp, grey morning teetering on the edge of June. Four miles will be sufficient to get us outside the Hurricane Zone but we are going to do a couple more - to Oriental. Within an hour and a half we are anchored.

We adore the place.

There is a stillness about it that is captivating. A stone breakwater protects the small harbour with its tiny fishing fleet in a far corner. And there is one of those waterfront houses, with a sloping lawn and shady tree, that you feel any troubled soul would look at and say, 'I could be happy there.' And after all the bad weather of the last few days it is now sunny and warm.

It is a limited anchorage in that it is small and shallow, and with a number of boats already anchored we are a bit closer to one of them - a small ketch called *Angel* - than we should have liked. As its owners pass in their dinghy, *Cherub*, we ask them if they are unhappy with our position because if they are we will move on to the next anchorage. They grin and say, 'After Memorial Day Weekend? This is *nothing*!'

They point out the tiny jetty which is the official dinghy dock and say if we walk in a straight line from there to the end of the block, and go into the chandlers on the right, they will lend us bicycles to get us to the supermarket.

'They're very cruiser friendly here,' says the wife.

On the left as you leave the harbour is a shop selling arts, craft and junk. It is a large, square, slightly worn wooden building, with a deep porch and fly screen, offering everything from old rocking chairs and pot plants to lamps and driftwood. And if anybody thinks America is a throw-away society they should go in there and think again.

The modern, spacious chandlery further along has things we've been seeking for months - especially a water filter for the galley sink - as well as some really good charts for Chesapeake, probably the best little bird book ever published, some inexpensive beer and some much-needed bungees.

The reason the bungees are needed speaks to the nature of bungees. We use ours mostly to anchor our cockpit awning to our side rails to stop it flapping. In strong wind or heavy rain we have to take down the awning.

This means releasing the bungees, which have a tendency to take advantage of even the slightest fumble of the fingers to fling themselves upwards, arc away from the boat and dive into the sea.

We leave our purchases to one side of the counter and pedal off into the village. The bicycles are a novelty: no gears and you pedal backwards to brake. But Oriental is perfectly flat and ideal for an indifferent cyclist like me. The friendly packer at the supermarket is a dead ringer for a young Bill Cosbie. And as I return the shopping cart after we've filled our rucksacks and cycle baskets outside, a woman my age holds the door open for me and says with the sweetest of smiles, 'Remember how it was, with the prams and pushchairs?'

Did we stumble, and fall into The Truman Show?

We take a couple of birthday cards across the road to the post office. The clerk is opening a large box of chocolates and setting it on the counter. He invites us to try them while he stamps our mail.

'Mmm,' I say. 'Nice. I'm not a great fan of nuts as a rule but these are lovely. What are they?'

'I don't know,' he says, lifting the box to read the ingredients label on the bottom. 'A customer brought them in.' He finds what he's looking for. 'Macadamia nuts,' he says.

'Good for the libido, apparently,' I tell him through the crunching.

'Really?' he says thoughtfully.

I nod, thinking that if I could only shift some of this pointless, randomly-acquired information that clutters up my brain I might actually find something useful in there.

He wishes us a really nice day as we leave, but as I turn at the doorway to reply, I see that he is already busy sliding the macadamia nuts back under the counter and lifting out a different box of chocolates to share with his customers.

Outside, two middle-aged women stand with a girl still in her teens. The latter is extending her hand to one of the older women, having just been introduced. 'I'm so happy to meet you at last,' she says with obvious pleasure. 'My mother has told me so much about you.'

Such grace in one so young. Maybe they're putting something in the water supply.

After lunch we go ashore again, for a wander round. This tiny harbour town has a network of small creeks behind it, although it faces the widest river in the USA, the Neuse. This in turn leads to the vast sailing waters of Pamlico Sound.

According to this year's census, the town's population is 875 making it, 'the largest city in the county.' It is an American habit to call a community, however small, a city. It undoubtedly has to do with incorporation and all sorts of other town council-type things like drains and street lighting, but also leaves one wondering if behind it may be a desire not to offend the folks who live there; that in a country where size matters the suggestion that you live in a village - or even a town - might imply some sort of inferiority.

The area was once the haunt of pirates, and Edward Teach, better known as Blackbeard, made his home just north of here. He is thought to have been one of the more gentlemanly of them, had been nice to his crew and is not known to have killed anybody wantonly, which sort of fits.

Oriental's wide streets have deep grass lawns in front of large, clapboard houses and little traffic. A laid-back youth with a girl on his handlebars cycles slowly past, one hand in his back pocket. A former cinema, now a community centre, doubles as a theatre. Arum lilies grow in front of the church. There is a duck pond, porches with rocking chairs and geraniums in pots, huge hydrangeas in the gardens and the perfume of early summer blossom.

A tiny chick, yellow and blue, with under-feathers sticking out from its head like ears, sits in the road. I pick him up and look into his determined little face. A thousand times smaller than me, he returns the look with confidence. I carry him to the grass verge out of harm's way, for his mother, hopping anxiously in a tree above us, to sort out. His tiny feet are warm and grasp my finger so tightly that I have to prise them off before I can put him down.

A woodpecker rat-tat-tats on a nearby tree trunk. I've heard woodpeckers and I've seen woodpeckers, but I've never seen one actually drilling a hole before. It's extraordinary. Like a miniature jack hammer, the sheer speed of the head takes your breath away.

Something that intrigues, if you are me anyway, is how such a quintessentially American town in North Carolina acquired the unlikely name of Oriental.

Until 1886, it seems, the little settlement was known as Smith's Creek after one of the waterways behind it, but in that year the US Post Office opened premises here. The wife of the newly-appointed postmaster, with a cavalier disregard for the community's history or opinion, renamed it Oriental from a nameplate washed up onto the beach from a wrecked steamship. If today's residents are anything to go by, this discourtesy would have been borne with fortitude.

Our cruising guide describes Oriental as 'Not picturesque'. Which is true. The simple act of trying to take a pretty picture of it defeats me, the place is so ordinary. Yet, even if it should be for this one day only, on *this* particular day at least it is the nicest, kindest, happiest, friendliest little town *ever*, in the entire history of the world. It is small town America as you always wanted it to be and never believed it could. I feel so happy and content I want to hug it.

'I think I'll retire here,' I tell David.

'Immigration won't let you,' he says.

22
Dismal Swamp or Virginia Cut?

As we prepare to leave next morning it soon becomes apparent that the 46-ft ketch anchored behind us is stuck in the mud. It has a much deeper keel than us, which is why it is stuck and we are still afloat. When we look at our depth gauge we see that, although there is normally only a 6-inch tide here, the water level has actually dropped two feet. A woman in the chandlers yesterday had told us they get wind-driven tides and that recently the water had risen as far as her doorstep.

We offer the owner of the ketch a tow. He comes out pretty easily and we both set off down the Neuse River into Pamlico Sound, which is fairly notorious for wind and chop but today is like a mill pond.

We get a call from the ketch owner to thank us for the tow and have a chat. His latest challenge is that the mud he churned up during his grounding has blocked the water cooling inlet to his refrigerator. He now has a well-heated refrigerator on what is becoming a very hot day.

Eight hours and 48 miles after leaving Oriental we anchor on the Pungo River. Just us and a shiny green and red coastal cruiser built like a miniature tug, complete with smoke stack and portholes.

We breakfast at dawn and begin lifting the anchor as the sun rises. It is a soft, still morning with a mist lying low and pale over the marshes and a blood-red sun rising behind the trees. Within a few hundred yards of leaving the anchorage we enter the canal that joins the Pungo and the Alligator Rivers. It is a narrow canal, dense with cypress forest on both sides and depending on your mood or disposition might be described as one of those secret places beloved by children, or a little claustrophobic.

The banks have been much eroded by the passage of boats which have washed the soil from the roots of the trees. It has left them gnarled and exposed, with some of them so like a book illustration by Arthur Rackham that you half expect to see a water nymph flitting through the undergrowth.

Trees with so much of their roots exposed reach a point where they no longer have the wherewithal to stay upright. Some are leaning against other trees, some lie horizontal and rotting in the mud providing not only a useful mulch for plants and creepers to establish their own roots in, but stumps and snags for the unwary boater.

Naturally, if you are going to meet a tug and barge coming the other way it will inevitably be somewhere this narrow. We move to the starboard bank to allow it to pass and hit the muddy bottom. As at Barefoot Landing, erosion has made the canal very shallow.

In the last few miles we have been travelling within sight of a yacht. As we approach Fairfield Swing Bridge, we hear the tender on the VHF asking its skipper if there is anyone behind him. We are not far behind, but obscured from the tender's view by a bend in the canal. The yacht's skipper says we are a long way back, adding 'They'll get the next opening.'

However, when we clear the bend at a minute before 7am the traffic on Highway 94 is still crossing the bridge so we increase our speed. But as we get within striking distance, the yachtsman calls the bridge irritably. 'Its four after seven! Will you be opening soon?'

The tender doesn't answer but as we close up sufficiently behind the other boat, the bells ring, the barriers come down, the bridge opens and the yacht goes through with us close behind it. The tender is outside his cabin on top of the bridge as we pass. We shout our thanks up to him and he waves. They are a special breed, these bridge operators: polite, calm, non-confrontational, determined to accommodate if they can do so without compromising safety, but impervious to bullying. Does the man make the bridge or the bridge the man? If the latter it could be an incomparable training ground for all sorts of things, including a better world. Sadly, the opening bridges are gradually being replaced by fixed ones, so the tenders are disappearing too.

At regular intervals there have been *For Sale* signs along the canal for plots of waterfront land and every now and again an area has been cleared and a caravan sits by the water's edge, for the owner to live in while the house is built. Such a home is the dream of many of us. But despite the great distances in this country you do begin to wonder if ultimately all the river bank, marshland and virgin woodland will disappear under real estate.

Mind you, the incomers here might have a bit of a fight on their hands if our own experience is anything to go by, because today we encounter the largest insects by far. They are BIG. One of them – black, furry and the size of a walnut - buzzes us persistently. We are afraid to swat it for fear of retaliation so we just duck every time it hurtles through the cockpit.

The water is very still and peaceful with nothing disturbing the surface ahead except where *Voyager*'s bows cut through it. Behind us the wash from our propellers is the colour of molten toffee being stirred in a pan. It comes from the peat out of which the canal has been cut. After the canal comes the Alligator River, described in the cruising guide as 'remote'. There is still cypress swamp on either side, but long sections of it are also extremely wide; miles wide, in fact.

Today is a 12-hour day. There is hardly a breath of wind and it is hot, but at least while you are on the move you are creating a breeze for yourself. The haze means you can only see as far as the next marker, about half a mile away. At Alligator River Bridge the female tender has a voice reminiscent of warm brandy before a blazing log fire and I can't do a thing with David for a good half hour afterwards.

Dragonflies flit across the cockpit. Dainty demoiselles, blue with a band on their tails, butt their heads delicately but repeatedly against the coaming. You wonder why they do it and if they get migraines. Half an hour after the bridge we are into the enormous Albemarle Sound.

Visibility is now very poor, the atmosphere heavy and the atmospherics decidedly odd as we become aware of unfamiliar engine noises vibrating through *Voyager*, although a quick check of her engines shows nothing amiss. Isolated as we are in a thick grey haze, we stand stock still, eyes wide but unseeing. The distant throbbing rises to a monstrous roar that suddenly explodes around us as a flight of Tomcat fighter planes thunder overhead, deafeningly loud and very low.

After recovering my wits, my first instinct is to wonder if they saw us as late as we saw them. But, of course, the average military cockpit is awash with state-of-the-art instrumentation including radar and, from my previous encounters with jet fighter planes, the pilots probably thought it would be great fun to home in on a distant target in a large and otherwise featureless stretch of water while scaring the living daylights out of a couple of unsuspecting yachtsmen in the process.

Ultimately there comes a point where you reach a marker buoy where you choose the route you want: to the Great Dismal Swamp Canal or to the Virginia Cut. The Dismal Swamp is described in *Skipper Bob* as the quieter and prettier of the two routes to Norfolk, the official end of the ICW. The Virginia Cut is shorter and quicker and has only one lock, whereas the Dismal Swamp has two which open only four times a day.

Initially we hesitate because the Swamp's route is not clearly marked on the charts with buoys, only compass bearings. But you can't pass up on something called The Great Dismal Swamp which at the same time is described as pretty, so as we cross the Albemarle Sound we bear left towards the Pasquotank River and Elizabeth City.

Way off to our right - though not visible today because of the haze - are the Outer Banks, the 200-mile long, slender curve of barrier islands lying off the North Carolina coast. It was on one of these islands, at a site called Kill Devil Hills in 1903 and making two flights each, that the Wright brothers, Orville and Wilbur, established the record for making the first powered and sustained heavier-than-air, pilot-controlled flight. The final one, by Wilbur, lasted 59 seconds and covered 852 feet.

They then walked four miles to the weather bureau in the little town of Kitty Hawk and telegraphed the news back home to their father in Dayton, Ohio. Their local newspaper declined to print the story, however, saying that the flight was too short to be important.

When a highly inaccurate article was published by a Virginia newspaper next day, the name Kitty Hawk – the source of the telegram - was reported as the site of the triumph and not the Kill Devil Hills campsite, four miles to the south, where it actually took place. And it was the name Kitty Hawk which went into the record and the history books and was subsequently bestowed on a US aircraft carrier, a stealth bomber, an aircraft transport ship and the Apollo 14 command module.

On the other hand, as a name to resonate and inspire, Kill Devil Hills is not the most user-friendly compared with the macho image of a bird of prey; not that there is such a bird as a kitty hawk. The name comes from a Native American word relating to hunting geese. Possibly.

It is surprising, in every culture, how much confusion, misinformation or alternative explanations surround even the most apparently straightforward events. Even quite recent ones. It really makes you wonder about the certainties of older, more hallowed histories.

It would be nice to visit both sites but it is just too hot for wandering about ashore at present and a treat better left for another time.

23
Elizabeth City

We began even earlier than usual this morning to benefit from the coolest part of the day. By mid-afternoon the temperature has passed 100°F in the shade. About an hour from Elizabeth City our port engine begins to belch smoke and we have to turn it off to let it cool. Both engines have been working steadily for hours on a long, very hot day.

Elizabeth City has a large water frontage and the approach to the harbour is very attractive; heavily wooded with lawns sweeping down to the river and some impressive-looking houses.

Work began on the Dismal Swamp in 1793 and by the early 19th century Elizabeth City had established itself as a centre of trade and commerce. The town today takes hospitality towards its visitors very seriously, not least its visiting boaters, providing fourteen free moorings for anyone staying 48 hours or less. As we near them we barely have time to realize that *Voyager* is too wide to fit between their piles when we see a man waving us towards a dock in front of a restaurant.

The man is Mr Lloyd who, with his wife and 86-year-old Fred Fearing are the Rose Buddies. They tie us up and invite us, and some other newly-arrived boaters, to a wine and cheese party on the restaurant's deck. They also present all the women in the party with a rosebud. It is a quite extraordinary welcome to a new town.

The Rose Buddies began in 1983, when Fred and his friend Joe Kramer threw an impromptu wine and cheese party on the waterfront for some visiting boaters. Then Joe, an avid rose grower, popped home and clipped a rosebud from his garden for each of the women and started a tradition. When Joe died, Mr and Mrs Lloyd stepped in to continue it with Fred.

We do the historical tour next morning, some nice old buildings and some very nice people. With the day rapidly beginning to heat up, we decide the supermarket is further away than we want to walk but find a handy food store of the old-fashioned kind. While the owner rings up our purchases he asks the inevitable question, 'Where ya from?'

Then, with that deadpan look of a thousand movies, he waves an arm around his no-frills little shop and says, 'Ya mean ya came all the way from England just to shop here?'

'Yep.'

'Well, I'll be,' he says, while his grin says he's nobody's fool. He offers us a ride back to the boat. We thank him but say not to leave his shop as we are fine with our rucksacks.

Close to home, so not far to carry it, a diner is selling take-out beer. It is very hot now and I have begun to droop, so while David waits at the counter I ask a customer if he minds my sitting at his table for a few minutes. My accent acts like a light switch. He had been with the US Air Force, based in Manchester in 1948 and part of the Berlin airlift. He grins at the memory of himself and three other flyers racing at the Bellevue Speedway until their base had stopped them because if personnel got hurt the USAF got left with the bills.

The waterfront restaurant does a very good lunch and afterwards a stiff onshore breeze comes up the river. This is very welcome to those of us already tied up here but not to the handful of small boats just arriving and trying to moor. They land sideways against the piles, lean against them for a while, maybe get a rope round one and swing off it, then try to reverse into the space between; pushing, shoving and shunting and partially dislodging a pile here and there.

Mostly, though, it doesn't occur to them to get out a rope or a fender until they are half-way in, or sideways on. So when you invite them to throw you a line so you can pull them in or tie them up, they say, 'Ah, a rope, I've got one somewhere,' and start hunting under cushions while their gelcoat scrapes against the piles.

In the evening there is a wedding party at the restaurant and dancing on the large dock beside us, during which a number of the guests stroll over for a chat, not least the Ring Bearer, escorted by his mother. A mere two years old he looks solemnly at the people still milling around in small boats attacking piles.

'Are all you people docking,' he asks, 'or are you about to go?' Told we will all be staying, he says, 'Oh,' disapprovingly and goes off to dance with the bride.

We leave our mooring with around ten other boats for the 9am opening of Elizabeth City's bascule bridge. We had thought to let them all go and take the next opening but word goes round that because of emergency repairs to the bridge it will not be opening again today until 5.30pm. As a result, we all start our engines too early, cast off too soon and then mill about in one another's way for ten minutes or more.

There are four parts to the bridge's opening section, each one lifting separately and *very* slowly - which is presumably why it needs emergency repairs. We are happy to go through last and the other boats are soon out of sight. The temperature has dropped considerably from yesterday and it looks as if it might even rain later.

The Pasquotank River, up to Elizabeth City, had been wide and relatively straight. On the other side of the bridge it begins to wind and twist, gradually getting narrower and narrower between overgrown banks as it makes its way through what is now the Great Dismal Swamp.

This may be its name, but the swamp is anything but dismal with its wild pink roses and the occasional magnolia among the white pine and cedars, trees with star-shaped leaves I couldn't put a name to, and dark green mistletoe. And full of birdsong. The water lilies are in yellow bud, and the smell of honeysuckle lulls the senses.

There is only the occasional small settlement along the way and a solitary man taking his morning exercise in a skiff. It is the first time we have ever seen an oarsman with a small rear-view mirror attached to his spectacles so that he can see where he is going. Or possibly a hungry alligator approaching from behind.

After about thirteen miles you leave the river and enter Turners Cut. The water here is a darker brown than ever. A 4-foot snake makes its way purposefully through it from one bank to the other, its body on the surface and its head a couple of inches above it, moving through the water the way a sidewinder does in the desert. The whole waterway has a drowsy, peaceful quality to it.

The Great Dismal Swamp once covered 2,000 square miles. It is sometimes said that George Washington surveyed it, but it seems that what he actually did was acquire 5,000 shares in a company that tried to drain it for farm land. It was not a successful venture, so instead its trees were cut down for shingles and other wood products, which turned out to be very profitable. Today it is reduced to 166 square miles but remains the largest protected swamp wilderness in the eastern United States.

Red wolves once roamed here, as they did throughout all the south-eastern States, but during the 1960s they were brought to the brink of extinction by forest clearances and predator control programmes. When the US Fish and Wildlife Service set out to capture as many as they could for a breeding programme they had to make do with only fourteen as the nucleus for their wilderness refuge. In 1988 the first cubs were born and wolves were gradually reintroduced into the wild.

After about four miles we arrive at South Mills Lock. The gates open at 1.30pm but it is an hour before the lock-keeper closes them again. This is largely because the first few boats that go in tie up to the lock walls in such a way that, although there is technically plenty of room for everybody, four of us are still outside. So the lock keeper has to make everybody already in the lock move forward so the rest of us can get in.

He is about to close the gates at last when a small, yellow-hulled sloop called *Chesapeake Duster* hoves into view, drifts very slowly towards the lock and then into the patch of water between *Voyager* and several boats rafted up on the opposite wall.

Initially undecided as to which side to tie up, the woman on deck finally looks expectantly at me.

'Got any fenders?' I ask.

'Yeh,' the woman on deck agrees dreamily.

'Want to tie some on?'

'Oh,' she says, frowning and calls to the man at the wheel, 'Do we have any fenders?'

After a search of their lockers she ties on a small fender and looks expectantly at me again.

'Got a rope?' I ask.

After another search, she emerges with one, tangled and too short to reach us anyway. But just as she makes a second throw, the helmsman - finding that by now he has drifted closer to the boats against the opposite wall than to us - guns his engine at one of them instead.

It soon becomes apparent that as well as having no mooring rope or fenders attached when they entered the lock, they don't have anything holding their boom in place either because, when they both go and stand on their side deck, their boat lurches over and their boom swings, knocking the people on the other boat for six. But finally the gates are closed.

The lock-keeper then goes round visiting every boat and writing down its name, registration number and draught. It is a slow-filling lock and much time might have been saved if he had opened the sluices before starting his list. However, having completed it, and opened the sluices, and waited until the water has slowly reached its limit, he then goes round every boat again and hands out an information booklet, which he could have done while he was writing down the details of all our boats or while the lock filled. It is after 3pm before the gates open again and there is another wait while he goes off to open the bascule bridge ahead of us.

Once you exit this lock you enter The Great Dismal Swamp Canal. Opened in 1805, and 22 miles long, it connects the Pasquotank River with the Elizabeth River just south of Norfolk, Virginia. It was conceived as an alternative to navigating the Outer Banks - scene of the Wright Brothers' flight – whose dangerous shoals and inlets have been responsible for the loss of many hundreds of ships.

Five miles along the canal we tie *Voyager* onto the outside of a large raft of boats at the North Carolina Welcome Station free dock. David goes off to the visitor centre for information while I prepare a meal.

After the heat of the last few days this evening is grey, wet and surprisingly cold and just the conditions, after a hot meal, to embark on Nathaniel Hawthorne's *The House of the Seven Gables*. A Gothic tale of murder and mystery, this mid-19th century novel tells of the remnants of a once-prosperous New England family descended from Puritans.

VIRGINIA

24
Norfolk

We are awake at our usual time. Nobody else is stirring, so we make our preparations quietly and slip off from the raft. As the last in, we have to leave first anyway, otherwise nobody else can. We also leave North Carolina here and enter Virginia. The weather continues cold and wet.

Ultimately a number of other boats catch up with us, happy for us to lead because they have a deeper draught than us. It is very shallow in places and we bottom ourselves once, avoiding a tree trunk in the water.

When we finally reach Deep Creek Bridge and Lock we tie up to a boat already waiting for the 11am opening and while David and its owner chat I pop down the road to the Food Lion. A cheerful woman at the Customer Service counter invites me to join their discount programme.

'If you have a card you get the discounts on special items,' she says. 'Just fill in this form.'

The problem becomes immediately obvious.

'I don't have an address and zip code,' I tell her.

'Ma'am?' she says.

'We're travelling through the US on a boat.'

'That's OK.'

'But what shall I put where it says address?'

'The Ocean!' She grins. Problem solved.

I return with fresh salmon and fruit, a box of teabags, Otis Spunkmeyer Muffins, a blueberry pie and a saving of $2.47 courtesy of my new discount card.

The lock is as slow-filling as yesterday's, but we are off again by noon; now out of the canal and into Deep Creek, which George Washington is said to have named after falling into it.

After about an hour of winding creek we reach the point where the Great Dismal Swamp and the Virginia Cut routes meet. We turn left into the Elizabeth River and under a series of bridges.

Two of them are railway bridges whose centres lift horizontally between two towers, instead of the usual drawbridge. On one of them a man with a bicycle asserts his constitutional right not to leave the bridge when asked to do so, and finally it rises with him and his bicycle still on it.

Two and a half miles further on we reach Norfolk and Portsmouth, one on either side of the river: Norfolk to starboard and Portsmouth to port.

Norfolk is Virginia's second largest city and given its strategic position has a long military history. The world's largest military alliance, the North Atlantic Treaty Organisation (NATO), has its North American headquarters here and it is home to the world's largest naval base of its kind. Norfolk, in short, is a navy town.

We are now on the edge of Chesapeake Bay and it isn't yet 2pm, but the day is so grey and dreary that we decide to stop anyway. We join a handful of other leisure boats at the Hospital Point anchorage, on the Portsmouth side of the river, directly below the big naval hospital.

The weather deteriorates further and we are grateful for the food purchased earlier. A hot tasty meal is especially enjoyable on a cold, wet day and we take great pleasure in poached salmon and hot blueberry pie.

After clearing the saloon table we spread out the material provided yesterday at the Welcome dock. That had been the first information centre of its kind we have encountered but the cities, and even quite small towns through which we've passed, have provided a very useful supply of information, ranging from maps, bus schedules, location of grocery stores and places of interest plus a little of the region's history.

Even the briefest scan of the present map makes me forget for a moment that I've left England at all, as familiar place names leap from the paper. Along with Portsmouth and Norfolk there is Hampton, Newport, Suffolk, Gloucester, Isle of Wight, Surrey and York. While something that strikes you, in local histories, is the way a new horizon gives a whole new direction to capable, energetic, hard-working people who feel they have few opportunities at home under current conditions.

One such person was Adam Thoroughgood (1604-1640) from King's Lynn in the English county of Norfolk. From a prominent family, but the ninth son, in 1622 he earned his passage to the Virginia colony as an indentured servant. When his term ended he returned to England, took a wife, and persuaded 105 settlers to return to the colony with him where he soon became a man of substance.

In 1634, when the colony was reorganised into a system of shires, Adam Thoroughgood gave the name of his home county to the area which later became the present-day city of Norfolk. And in return for attracting such a large number of settlers he was given extensive lands along the Lynnhaven River, which he named after his former home at King's Lynn.

One of his original 105 settlers, another Norfolk man called Augustine Warner, became an ancestor of both the future George Washington and Robert E Lee.

A new day dawns grey, windy, cold and wet. So after breakfast we go back to bed until coffee time. Determined that David will have a flavour of American literature in its own homeland I continue reading Nathaniel Hawthorne's *The House of the Seven Gables* to him. But with its themes of guilt and retribution, and depression spiralling down into madness, it would have a lowering effect even in bright sunshine. On a grim day like this one it is sending us over the edge.

I have been asking, rhetorically, for some time now why so many significant novels of literary merit have to be so profoundly depressing. I mean, if Austen and Tolstoy can explore the moral universe with wit and humour, why can't a few other people? For this reason I suspect that David has hidden the new copy of Virginia Woolf, which I've been reading to myself, until the weather is more uplifting. The forecast is not encouraging, however. I have to keep reminding myself that this is June. The wind howls all night.

There is another sound to this place. Lively or mournful, depending on whether it's raining or you're reading *The House of the Seven Gables* or not. It is the sound of tugboat horns and they must remain in the memory of patients long after they have left the hospital up on the bank behind us. They are already embedded in mine. Tugboats pushing huge barges, sometimes six at a time - three in a line and two-abreast. And definitely not something you'd look forward to meeting coming the other way on a winding section of waterway.

25
To Chesapeake Bay

When you leave Hospital Point you say farewell to the ICW. There is a dotted line on the chart, between Norfolk and Portsmouth, which represents an imaginary line marking the northern extreme of the ICW, although you are still on the Elizabeth River. You are also still in a narrow, marked channel as the river either side of it is shallow.

On the Norfolk side you pass what seem like endless dockyards filled with Navy ships, some being refitted and some decommissioned. All to the accompaniment of a great clanging, clattering and hammering until you enter the very wide waterway of Hampton Roads where three rivers meet on the Portsmouth side. One of them is the James River, and 35 miles up it is the site of the first permanent English settlement in America, founded in 1607 and named Jamestown after the Scottish king who had inherited the throne of England and Ireland four years earlier from the childless Elizabeth.

Crossing Hampton Roads we stay out of the main shipping channel, between the Atlantic and Norfolk, to avoid obstructing a number of large vessels heading towards the Elizabeth River. These include two Navy destroyers, a bulk carrier and a tug pushing a very long barge. One of the destroyers is repeatedly calling up a small yacht which, despite plenty of depth on the outside of the channel is not only sailing up the inside of it but doing so on the wrong side.

Its skipper is perhaps assuming that power must give way to sail while ignoring the fact that this doesn't apply where a large vessel is restricted by the limitations of a channel and its ability to manoeuvre. Or maybe he's just not looking where he's going because as we get closer - and with the destroyer still trying to persuade him to answer his VHF - we can see that the shipping hazard in question is none other than *Chesapeake Duster*, from South Mills Lock the other day. Its skipper's refusal to move out of the way finally results in the Navy ship coming to a halt in front of its sister ship to avoid a collision with the yacht.

Having kept out of the main shipping channel ourselves for as long as possible, we reach a point where we must now cross it if we are to continue our journey north. There is still a lot of traffic, and things are further complicated by a Navy vessel slowing down to let a container ship overtake it. But once safely across, we finally enter Chesapeake Bay.

At around 200 miles long it is the largest estuary in the USA. It is bordered by two States - Virginia and Maryland - and has more than 150 rivers and streams feeding into it. It is also one of America's most famous sailing areas, blessed with picturesque towns and villages, sheltered anchorages, all the crab you can eat and a major objective of this voyage.

As a change from so many English towns and counties, the name Chesapeake is derived from a Native American word belonging to one of the Algonquian tribes and referring to a village at a big river.

Algonquian languages were among the first that Europeans encountered on arriving in North America, and many of their words have found their way into English, including toboggan, moccasin and skunk. The names of eastern and mid-western States, such as Connecticut, Massachusetts, Illinois and Michigan, are also of Algonquian origin along with the cities Chicago and Milwaukee.

From now on all is quiet and relaxed. The water is also deep enough for us to ignore the channel markers - which are intended for large seagoing ships only - and go wherever we want. So we put up the genoa and sail. It is a delight to be in open water again.

There is little other traffic, all of it distant apart from a passing clanker, and that only very briefly. This non-technical term derives from a small sloop that anchored close to us off the south coast of England some years ago. Virtually everything on it had clattered and rattled throughout the entire blustery night. Staring resentfully at its nameplate, *Kalinka*, next morning a sleep-deprived David had said sourly, 'I think that should be *Klanka*,' and all such boats became clankers.

The current one is a 33-foot cutter-rigged ketch which overtakes us with its engine roaring and its sails flapping and flogging. Above its foredeck an anchor ball clatters against the rigging, while two large fenders hanging over its starboard beam bump against its topsides. With such ill-usage it must be a noisy, vibrating, stressful boat to travel on and seriously at odds with the name on its transom: *Tranquillity*.

After a cool, bright sunny morning, the afternoon becomes warm and rather hazy. There is a wonderful languor to it and no-one in sight; just the deep, slow voice of a boater over the VHF calling periodically, '*Snoopdoggy*. This is *Rowboat*.'

Visibility begins to decline as the afternoon progresses. Our cruising guide has warned us to look out for Chesapeake dusters, the violent squalls common to the bay and which can suddenly overwhelm an unsuspecting yachtsman. What it hasn't said anything about is strange encounters. As visibility continues to deteriorate we are startled to find ourselves surrounded by grey, medium-sized, anonymous-looking vessels. There are seven of them, each with a large dinghy on davits hanging over both quarters, and not going anywhere, just drifting around. As we sail on, more of them become visible in the gloom.

We find it bewildering, especially when one of us comments that there appears to be no-one on board any of these boats, and then men suddenly appear. As we approach the next group we remark that the people sitting on deck are not moving at all, perhaps they're dummies, and they turn their heads. We whisper about parabolic listening devices and Scully and Mulder and concentrate our energies on finding tonight's anchorage.

Fishing Bay is just inside the mouth of the Piankatank River. It is well-marked and easy to enter for our first Chesapeake Bay anchorage, especially in the misty conditions of this late afternoon. It is well protected from north, east and west winds and the cruising guide makes a point of the fact that it is 'mosquito free'. When something like this is specifically mentioned, you do tend to wonder what everywhere else is like.

The mist disappears soon after our arrival and, as well as a mosquito-free evening, we are rewarded with a lovely sunset. So, with sea trout and fresh vegetables simmering on the stove, we open a bottle of wine and celebrate our first day in Chesapeake.

POTOMAC
AND
DISTRICT OF
COLUMBIA

26
Potomac River

We up-anchor at 6.45am. After the chilly last few days the forecast is for 90°F plus, and humid. Even this early it is already warm and it will be a long day – 60 miles and more than twelve hours.

During the course of the morning we see the grey ships again, and come over all paranoid, wondering if they are the marine equivalent of the 'greys' beloved by alien abduction theorists. But, like yesterday's, they do not seem to be going anywhere and are soon left behind.

We want to visit the nation's capital and to do it now rather than on our way back south. So in the afternoon we leave Chesapeake Bay, turn left into the Potomac River and begin the 105-mile journey to Washington. The mouth of the Potomac is very wide. Depending on where you place your dividers on the chart you can make it anything from five to ten miles. It is also one of Chesapeake's biggest tributaries, its waters travelling 400 miles from up in the mountains of West Virginia.

'Potomac' is derived from another Algonquian name, that of a tribe which once inhabited the river's upper reaches. Shown as Patawomeke on the map of Captain John Smith (the explorer whose life was famously saved by Pocahontas), the unromantic-sounding Board On Geographic Names officially declared it Potomac in 1931.

The day becomes hot and hazy. For a while the channel markers are visible only a short distance ahead and the shores of this very broad river can't be seen at all. When we do finally glimpse one, there are some stunning houses with a sandy beach in front and forest behind. The current is against us most of the way and as expected, we make less than five knots, eventually arriving at St Clements Island around 7pm.

St Clements Island is where Maryland's first colonists landed in 1634 on their two ships, the *Ark* and the *Dove,* which also served as a temporary base while they negotiated with the Yaocomico Tribe for land on which to build a permanent settlement.

The new arrivals named it for St Clement, the martyr cast into the sea with an anchor round his neck. At that time the island measured almost 400 acres but today extends to only forty. This uninhabited island is now a State park and nature reserve accessible only by boat. It has a generous length of free dock, although we are the only boat tied up on it. We walk a short distance into the island, with its 40-foot memorial cross commemorating the first Marylanders, and the place looks very attractive.

Shadows are lengthening, however, and it has been a long, hot day. Even that would not normally have put us off exploring the island a little further if David and I had not felt so ill at ease. Intuition is a strange thing and usually it is just me, but this evening even David is uncomfortable. We both feel, however irrationally, that we are being watched and when we get back to *Voyager* we untie her and go out to anchor for the night.

Next morning we have the engines on at 5.30 so as to reach our next destination in daylight. As David takes *Voyager* out, I turn to take a last look at the island. Although there is no sign of any other boat, and despite the earliness of the hour, there is a man standing on the dock. He neither smiles nor waves, but simply stares after us. He may have been entirely harmless. But something you learn to do when there are just the two of you in isolated places is to trust your instincts.

Today is Saturday. The plan is to reach the Woodrow Wilson Memorial Bridge at the entrance to Washington by this evening so that we can catch its final opening early on Sunday morning. Because the level of road traffic in and out of the nation's capital is so intense during the day, the bridge remains closed to shipping from 5am to midnight Monday to Friday. At weekends, however, its closing time is from 7am until midnight and those two extra hours of opening time between 5am and 7am enable you to navigate the last five miles up the Potomac River to the city and anchor in daylight.

If we miss tomorrow's dawn opening there will not be another in daylight for five days. Accordingly we have done longer passages than usual in the last couple of days and plan to anchor south of the bridge tonight so that we can go through on the last opening tomorrow morning.

Another very hot and humid day is forecast, along with warnings for neighbours to keep an eye on those at risk, such as senior citizens and children. By 8am the promised heat has arrived. The weekend boaters, surprisingly, have not. In fact, all is quiet until 1 o'clock when everybody, it seems, with access to a boat materializes on the river.

The temperature reaches 104°F in the shade by mid-afternoon. The green algae floating on its surface makes the river look rank and sullen and a number of large fish float past lying on their sides. It seems they die from a lack of oxygen in the water when it gets this hot.

Like everywhere else, ospreys are present wherever a channel marker is available. In Florida there were well-advanced chicks a month ago. Up here they are still building their nests. The most touching among them is a pair trying to build one in the 12-inch gap between the two boards of one of the most basic types of marker post. Not surprisingly they are having no luck.

This is clearly their first attempt at nest-building. The female, crouched over half a dozen twigs, is cheeping plaintively. The male carries the wrong size stick to her which she takes from him but, as she tries to fit it in the small space available, it falls in the water. After retrieving it a couple of times, it sinks before he can catch it and he flies for the shore to get another one.

Their pitiable situation is highlighted by the next channel marker post along, which is a most substantial affair. There is not only a battery platform to provide stability for the nest but even a small rail around it, reminiscent of a picket fence. And within it sits a nesting female which, if you could ever ascribe such an expression to the mournful features of an osprey, looks almost smug.

We spot the Wilson Bridge around 5.15pm and call up the tender to confirm that there will in fact *be* a 7am opening tomorrow, and if so to book our passage through it - something you are required to do twelve hours in advance. He tells us the last opening will be at 6.30am.

Then we settle into the anchorage at Smoot's Cove, not far from the bridge. There is the most wonderful smell of blossom from somewhere and it is very peaceful. Meantime, out on the windless river, small yachts and sailing dinghies - their skippers imbued with the true sailor's determination to make it home under sail whatever the conditions - barely move except when a small powerboat rips through them, its passengers the colour of cooked lobster after a day under a broiling sun.

The banks are wooded and very green. Sunset is liquid gold. Sometime after 9pm, and with both of us horizontal in the saloon, we are drawn up on deck by loud bangs as if something is attacking our hull. I don't know how many years it takes before you automatically recognise the effect of sound travelling through water.

The attack on us is in fact a spectacular Welcome to Washington fireworks display just the other side of the bridge. It is absolutely gorgeous with the most stunning finale we have ever seen - a bouquet of flowers created out of exploding light.

It turns out to be a bouncy night filled with the sound of engines. Some of them are planes overhead but mostly they are small boats travelling down the river, presumably people returning from Washington restaurants and parties to riverside homes south of the bridge. For what better way to travel from a busy city centre on a summer Saturday night than by boat on an uncongested, traffic-cop-free river? *Voyager*'s hull sets up a constant hum from them, and there is the occasional thump as items we forgot to lay down before going to bed fall over in the wash.

The Wilson Bridge was opened in 1961 and named in honour of Woodrow Wilson, elected 28th US President in 1912. It spans the shores of two States, Maryland and Virginia, and was designed in the late '50s for an estimated 75,000 vehicles a day. However, thanks to a variety of complex and unforeseen reasons, by the year 2000 it is handling 200,000 a day. It is the only river-crossing south of Washington and as such is part of Interstate 95 as well as the Washington Beltway.

Not least of the problems is that the highway at both ends of it has been widened to eight lanes, turning the six-lane bridge into a bottleneck. Not surprisingly, as well as limiting the number of openings, the aim is to keep each one as brief as possible to prevent traffic hold-ups.

So, before going to bed we work out the timing for getting to the bridge tomorrow morning in good order. It is currently taking us twenty minutes to raise our anchor (including removing a great deal of mud from it) and, as we are about a mile from the bridge, say another fifteen minutes. Add a bit to be on the safe side and we plan to start 45 minutes before the bridge opening.

Neither of us can remember the last time the anchor came up so quickly and easily. It takes a little under six minutes. Not mud here, but gravel. We set off anyway and when we get to the bridge we hover, and have breakfast watching an incredible red sun rise behind an osprey staring down at a half-built nest with that acute sense of failure common to so many of them. For a while, the whole sky and river are deepest red.

David rings the bridge tender at 6.10 to say that we are standing by for the 6.30 opening. Shortly afterwards the process of clearing traffic from its one-and-a-quarter-mile span begins. When it opens, it lifts in four pieces. As you pass underneath you enter the third State encompassed by this bridge, District of Columbia, or DC for short, founded in 1791 to serve as the new national capital and independent of all other US States.

27
Washington

We have the most wonderful sail up the Potomac River to Washington. At this time on a Sunday morning we have it all to ourselves apart from a mallard duck with nine young. For some unaccountable reason she aims her brood straight at our port bow and David ends up swerving to avoid mowing them down.

Initially there is a river mist and visibility is limited so I go up on the foredeck to look for channel marker buoys. When the red sun has risen sufficiently, the mist evaporates but I stay where I am anyway because, suddenly, you are physically entering the political and military heart of America.

The US Naval Research Laboratory is to our right and, as if in counterpoint, two square-riggers are moored on our left; they are en route to the Tall Ships Festival at New York's Fourth of July celebrations before going on to Europe. A short distance further on, and with something of a shock, I realize that I am looking at the distinctive shape of the Pentagon.

And out there, all around us, some hidden behind the trees, are the names one knows so well. Langley, where the CIA hang out. Arlington, the national military cemetery. Bethesda naval hospital, which became familiar worldwide from President Kennedy's visits there. The Naval Observatory, the Washington Navy Yard and the US Naval Station.

Meanwhile way ahead of us, above the trees and visible for every bit of the journey, is the great central dome of the United States Capitol, where the US Congress - the legislature of the US federal government - meets. One reason the view is so spectacular is that in 1910 DC outlawed skyscrapers.

At the airport there is a fork in the river, with the Potomac going off to the left and the Anacostia River to the right. In between them is an inlet called the Washington Channel which has an island to port, and the mainland - with a small marina on it - to starboard. This channel also provides a long, narrow anchorage on the very edge of the city centre.

Once settled, and as required, we call up the harbour-side Police on the VHF and are invited to come over, 'at your leisure,' as Officer Price very graciously puts it. We dinghy in. It is a place of giants. The three officers on duty are probably the tallest men I have ever seen, and their office is of a size to accommodate them. Accordingly I peer over the top of a counter that comes up to my collar bone, but when Officer Price gets up from his chair and walks over to us, it is normal size to him. He is very helpful. Especially concerning our most pressing problem - trash. There are bins around, he says. Distribute it discreetly. Or we have a dumpster.

We leave wondering why this huge office, with only three men in it, is full to the gunnels with crates of soft drink. It is stashed everywhere - on shelves, under desks, against walls. When we get back to the dinghy our five bags of trash rise up to meet us.

After marinating out in the sun in 120 degrees for several days they shimmer in a stench that has become indescribable. We carry them ... discreetly ... past Officer Price's window, through the gate saying No Entry, Police Personnel Only, and put them in the Police dumpster. It is very fresh in there, containing as it does only soft drink cans and polystyrene cups. They are going to notice a difference. Our dinghy still smells even when the bags have gone and it has been thoroughly washed.

Although we don't like using a second anchor we put one out, because Officer Price has asked us to. The inlet, he warned, is subject to 30-40mph squalls of up to an hour's duration which sometimes sends boats into the wall. The wall referred to is the one surrounding the island beside us, which is a golf course and recreation area and beautifully landscaped.

In fact, this is a most attractive place to be. As well as the delightful island beside us, *Voyager* currently lies facing the Washington Monument and the 14th Street Bridge plus at least four others, so there is a vista of diminishing bridges with road and rail traffic criss-crossing the Potomac. Train whistles echo over the water towards us, and truck horns; some assertive, some mournful and one which sounds like Jimmy Durante's *Lost Chord*, although you have to be over a certain age to appreciate that one. They are particularly evocative at night, wailing in the darkness, with the two red lights on the apex of the Washington Monument - to alert aircraft to the obelisk's presence - blinking on and off like two mad eyes.

Monday morning we dinghy ashore just after 7am, with the day just beginning and still deliciously cool from an overnight shower. Our route takes us through the seafood market with its mountains of prawns, lobsters, langoustine - and pretty much any other crustacean you can think of - on groaning trestles either side of us. The signs saying 'cooked hot crab' make our mouths water, even so soon after breakfast. Something to enjoy later. For now, we are off to see the sights.

A capital city is a nation's showcase for its great men, its military and political power, its culture and its collections. Our first stop is at the neo-classical building dedicated to Thomas Jefferson (1743–1826) a Founding Father, the principal author of the Declaration of Independence and the third President of the United States. So we are surprised to discover that construction on the Jefferson Monument was not begun until 1939 and that his bronze statue was only finally put in place within our own lifetime. But then, getting a monument depends on who your friends or admirers are (in this case, President Roosevelt). Or, just as importantly, who your enemies are.

Not even George Washington was immune. We walk up a small incline for a closer look at the obelisk we can see from *Voyager*. Hailed as the father of his country and the dominant military and political leader of the new United States of America - and its first inaugurated President - George Washington exemplified his country's central ideals of republican virtues, civic duty and patriotism. Yet within two years of his death in 1799 the Jeffersonian Republicans, then in control of Congress, blocked plans to build a memorial to him, put his image on the coinage or even allow his birthday to be celebrated.

Work finally began on the 555-feet tall Washington Monument in 1848, but stopped again between 1854 and 1877. The hiatus can be seen in a small change in the colour of the marble about 150 feet up. Among the causes of this delay was further political bickering - one of the more reactionary forces being the far-right and interestingly-named Know Nothing Party. The memorial officially opened in 1885, nearly a century after the proposal to build one was first made.

One source of delay, of course, was the Civil War. The most heart-breaking image for me is of a group of infantrymen, calmly writing their names and addresses on slips of paper and pinning them to the backs of their uniforms. The soldiers hoped this would enable somebody to let their families at home know what happened to them. Exhausted and facing overwhelming odds, they were about to be marched into a barrage of musket and cannon fire and knew that little of their fronts would be left to identify them.

Of all wars, the most bitter is the civil kind. Two weeks ago we sailed past the place where America's officially began, Fort Sumter in Charleston Harbour, South Carolina. Our next stop this morning is the commemoration of the man who not only brought that war to an end but prevented the Union from disintegrating. In the process he also managed to outlaw the slavery underpinning its divisions.

To get to the Lincoln Memorial you walk under the shade trees beside its long, rectangular Reflecting Pool. Depending on your vantage point, the pool reflects the Lincoln Memorial in one direction or the Washington Monument in the other.

At present we have the reflection of the Lincoln Memorial ahead of us, and soon that great statue of the seated President itself. It is housed in a massive Greek temple – far too grand for such a humble man, it was argued when the plans were initially unveiled and the inevitable squabbling began – but somehow you don't notice the temple until later. You simply climb the steps, as if drawn by some invisible thread, and stand looking up at the enormous statue. If anything it seems even larger than it did in that old black and white James Stewart movie, *Mr Smith Goes To Washington,* in which a provincial Senate replacement finds himself taking on political corruption in the nation's capital.

Originally intended to be only 10 feet high, from shoes to crown the seated figure of Abraham Lincoln, 16th President of the United States of America, is 19 feet high and a similar width. It was carved from Georgia marble by the sons of an Italian immigrant from Carrara in Tuscany, a place famous for its marble quarries and carvers.

Although the monument was first proposed in 1867, construction did not begin until 1914 with its opening to the public in 1922. Looking so venerable, as it now does, and almost eternal in its massive stillness, it is a shock to realize that when James Stewart stood before it in the role of a beleaguered young senator, the entire edifice was barely 17 years old.

On its south and north walls are Lincoln's two most famous speeches. Both of them refer to freedom and equality but especially to the importance of union. There is again concern about America dividing into two, only this time between English and Spanish speakers. Increasingly, public information and signage has to be provided in both languages.

From the Civil War we move on to more recent confrontations. For a capital is also where those who died for their country are honoured. The memorial to the Korean War (1950–1953) is a group of 19 statues depicting a squad on patrol. Behind it is a black granite wall with several thousand photographs of troops sandblasted onto it so that their faces seem to loom up at you out of the stone. You are struck by their eyes. And their youth. The Korean death toll was over 54,000 Americans.

The nearby Vietnam memorial is dominated by two long walls engraved with the names of the fallen from the first in 1959, to the last in 1975. One wall points towards the Washington Monument, the other to the Lincoln Memorial. While the larger than life-size figures of the Korean memorial humanize - faces, expressions and roles, especially the one at the rear with bulky equipment on his back and his cape over it to keep off the rain - the Vietnam monument speaks of the scale of the loss - more than 58,000 US troops killed or missing in action. Although Korean losses were similar, the bare numbers on its plaque could never have the same impact as all those names.

Nearly five million Americans also fought in World War I, and over 16 million served in World War II. Yet you have to look for a mark of their sacrifice in their home States. At this time there is no national memorial to the fallen of either war in Washington.

From the Korean and Vietnam war memorials the White House is just a short walk away through an area of green space called The Ellipse. It has gratings in the grass emitting steam, which gives a strange effect to the back of the presidential building. Round the front you are struck by how small it appears from the road, more like a country gentleman's residence than a presidential palace.

In front of the railings an enterprising photographer has propped a life-size cardboard cut-out of the present incumbent, and anyone so inclined can have their photograph taken alongside President Clinton with the White House as a backdrop. No respecter of persons, the American entrepreneur.

We are too late to get a tour of the building today. So we continue on down Pennsylvania Avenue, past The Treasury and through an interesting cross-section: the Warner Brothers store, FBI Building, US Navy memorial, Department of Justice, National Archives and the National Gallery of Art, West Building.

In the latter there is an exhibition of 17th and 18th century architects' models. They are exquisite, very detailed and intricate, with the one for the London church of St Martin in the Fields in Trafalgar Square complete right down to its tiny pews. The church's architect would have had this made from his plans, not only to show the church commissioners what the final building was going to look like but also as an aid for the builder during its construction.

Next day it is back down the National Mall, this time to the Smithsonian Institution's huge complex of galleries and museums. We particularly enjoy the Freer, not least an exhibition entitled *Picturing Whistler*, containing portraits and self-portraits of and by the 19th century American artist James McNeill Whistler. So often less is more, and some of the small pencil sketches are superb.

Another treat is the Air & Space Museum. In pride of place is the Wright *Flyer*, the first powered, heavier-than-air machine to achieve controlled sustained flight with a pilot aboard. Just over a week ago we passed North Carolina's barrier islands, the site of its record-breaking flight. The *Flyer* itself is made from spruce and, because no suitable automobile engine could be found, was powered by one that borrowed from bicycle technology. The pilot lay on his stomach to reduce drag and steered by moving a cradle attached to his hips. It is sobering to reflect, however, that from achieving a flight of only 852 feet and less than a minute in 1903, barely twelve years later flying machines had become weapons of war.

There are a lot of Firsts here. Like the *Spirit of St Louis*, the tiny single-engine, single-seater plane in which Charles Lindbergh made the first non-stop flight from New York to Paris in May 1927. You are struck by its apparent fragility. The fuselage's frame is made of metal tubes and the wing frames of wood, and both are covered in fabric. All designed to minimize weight. What particularly caught my eye was the pilot's wicker-work seat.

Also celebrated is the first man-pedal-powered plane; Breitling Orbiter 3, the first balloon to circumnavigate the earth; Bell X-1, the first plane to fly faster than the speed of sound; a replica of Sputnik, the first manned spacecraft; the first spacewalk; and the 1969 Lunar module which made the first moon landing. The last looks surprisingly home-made, like a combination of lightweight DIY scaffolding and tinfoil. And so cramped it must have been a relief to get out and stretch the legs.

There are also some marvellous exhibitions around town. African American photographers. Salvador Dali. Dutch Masters: Rembrandt, Franz Hals and Vermeer. And Gerrit Dou, who studied with Rembrandt and whose domestic scenes and portraits have the quality of still-life.

Normally, collections contain two or three. It is a rare treat to see more than a dozen gathered together.

In between cultural pursuits I take our laundry ashore. I have just committed four loads to the marina's washers when the owner arrives and says all the machines (four washers and four dryers) are about to be removed. The dryers have already gone by the time our laundry is out of the washers. But with the temperature currently in the 90s it soon begins to dry pegged out on *Voyager's* side rails.

It is muggy today, as well as hot, so every hatch on the boat is open when the sky in the north-west turns purple and then black. We race to batten down before the deluge begins and just manage to get the laundry in before a most extraordinary wind can carry it away.

Voyager spins round, drags up both anchors and begins rushing backwards towards the Canadian yacht behind us. Poor David is out on the bow in torrential rain hauling up and unravelling two anchors while I hold us off several other dragging boats and the park wall. The squall lasts around 45 minutes.

A regular visitor throughout our stay is a fleet of presidential helicopters, with an occasional helicopter gunship in attendance, which flies up the Washington Channel only a short distance above our masthead. During one flyover a single-portion paper cup, half full of tomato ketchup, lands on our afterdeck and we wonder if the other half of the contents had just graced the presidential burger.

On one of the days we dig out our dinghy's sailing gear and rig it up for a sail down the Washington Channel, under the 14th Street Bridge and into the Tidal Basin.

A quick glance at a chart before setting out reveals a familiar name off the north-western edge of the basin. Names fascinate and none more so than this one - Foggy Bottom - because I have only ever heard it used in reference to the US Department of State and had always taken it to be a facetious nickname inflicted by the media on a government department with a need for circumspection in its public statements.

So I am fascinated to find that it is a real place, a late-18th century historical district and one of the oldest in Washington. Originally industrial and working class, as well as the fog caused by its low-lying riverside location, it probably owed its name to the smoke given off by nearby breweries, glass plants and the city gas works.

Nowadays Foggy Bottom is home not only to the State Department but many other famous institutions as diverse as George Washington University, the Kennedy Centre for Performing Arts and the infamous Watergate complex, the burglary of which resulted in the resignation of President Richard Nixon.

On the return trip it takes a bit of effort to get back onto *Voyager*. Because of the wind, she keeps swinging away every time we try to grasp her stern handrail. In the end we resort to dropping the dinghy's sail and paddling the last few yards.

In the park opposite a family has set up trestle tables and a barbecue. The charcoal has just reached that stage of perfection when the sky closes in and produces a deluge. We watch in horror as the family, plus numerous golfers and joggers, all shelter confidently under the trees amid frequent bolts of lightning, despite the well-documented evidence of fatalities among people sheltering under trees during thunder storms. But after this one has passed over, everyone appears to have survived.

As well as monuments, museums, embassies, hotels and government buildings Washington is a city of transients of one kind or another; out-of-towners either legislating or doing the sights, with the people who service it commuting from many miles away, and the *Washington Post* using phrases like, '...if we are to encourage residents back into the city.' But as two of those transients, and despite the heat and occasionally violent squalls, we have had a terrific week here.

It is Sunday morning again and we start the engines at 5.30 to make the last daylight opening of the Woodrow Wilson Bridge. It is a heron morning. They are all around us with their massive wings and languid flight.

The bridge opens easily enough but, after we've passed through, it fails to close again, two of its four lifting sections remaining obstinately open. In a land where celebrity status is all-encompassing, it would be flattering to think that for a few moments at least we had brought the nation's capital to a standstill. But at 6.45 on a Sunday morning you've got to be realistic.

28
A Different World

The change in our surroundings in the following days could not be more dramatic as we leave the bustle and sheer monumentality of Washington for the quiet coves and secluded creeks of the Potomac. At Coles Point, we anchor in a beautiful, tranquil bay.

Shopping habits change, too. After the city's giant supermarket we now dinghy over to Branson Cove's little store and café with its large, wood-burning stove in the centre and a pool table behind the shelves. A sign on the door offers live bait – 'blood worms, red wigglers and night crawlers'. They are kept in a designated refrigerator but for the non-angler, not to mention the slightly squeamish, there is a touch of horror associated with opening the wrong door and finding that lot shuffling about inside.

We buy a few items, but the post office we need is on the other side of the creek. On the opposite bank we pass large glass tanks where blue crabs are kept in controlled water temperatures until they shed their shells and become ready for the table as soft-shelled crabs.

After the post office we decide to have a look at the nearby nature trails. A man stops and offers us a lift. He turns out to be the owner, and when we get there he takes us into the shop, gives us maps and postcards and points us in the right direction. We walk for miles, under tall trees, down leafy paths in cool green shade, beside pools where small terrapin scuttle for cover at our approach and water snakes sidle by. We emerge several hours later surprised at the sheer brightness of the day.

We lunch in the Driftwood restaurant on crab cakes, soft-shelled crabs, fried fish and oysters. Then buy bread and pound cake from a store which is straight out of a Norman Rockwell painting, with the proprietor's rocking chair beside the stove, a round-cornered 1950s fridge, and a cat sleeping on its side on a window ledge with its feet dangling over the edge. Time has little relevance here.

Only as we return to the dinghy, do we remember that we left food in it from the first store we stopped at and which will have been spoiled in the heat. But just as time appears to run at a different speed here, so the environment seems to have a thoughtful turn to it. Either wind or tide has carried our dinghy underneath the jetty, keeping the boat and everything inside it blissfully cool.

We wake next morning to the sound of osprey – a sharp, slightly annoyed whistle – but which seems unusually close. Thinking we must have dragged towards the shore we rush up on deck but find instead that two of them have decided *Voyager* will make a suitable nesting site.

The male is on the top of our mast balancing on the navigation light – we hope it will still work when we next need it - and the female is slipping and sliding on the radar scanner wondering how to get her twigs to stay put long enough to become a nest.

We shoo them away so they can use their energy to build with some hope of success and, with twigs falling around us, set off down the last part of the Potomac River and out into Chesapeake Bay.

MARYLAND

29
Quiet Places

Our anchorage for the night is Mill Creek, about half a mile from the town of Solomons Island and at the mouth of the Patuxent River. It is very pretty with just a scattering of clapboard houses, piers and pontoons and the regular cry of osprey which of course are nesting on every available marker post.

Solomons Island isn't an island at all but a triangle of land joined to the mainland by a substantial causeway. An old building in the village turns out to be a small fishing museum and the lovely man on the door introduces himself as Marshall Bailey, an ex-crabber. He is an excellent guide to the old implements around the walls and the fishing techniques needed to use them. Then he seats us in a small projection room to watch a film made in the 1950s.

This museum had once been the processing plant where some of the film was shot. Shelled oysters are being put into cans which, in the days before refrigerated trucks, are then put into barrels packed with ice for delivery to the cities.

The flickering black and white film's most captivating images, however, are of the skipjacks under sail - boats that are themselves now museum pieces - dredging the oyster beds out in the bay.

Back outside we spot a man getting into a station wagon and ask directions to the shops. He points and says, 'About half a mile,' and drives away. We figure we'll do about a mile and then ask again. If it's going to be too far we can always have cheese for lunch.

Within minutes he returns, pulls up alongside and offers us a lift, having realized from our sailing jackets that we won't have a car. He had married an English girl from Hendon in North London during the war, he tells us. Sadly she had recently died but her mother, who is 97, continues to live in her own home and he had just visited her. The memories tumble forth.

In town we buy snow crab claws, scallops and what Americans call shrimp despite being the size of a large prawn, all of which they then steam for us.

'How do you want 'em? Mild, medium or hot spiced?'

Then, quite unasked, a woman materializes from somewhere in the store and drives us back to our dinghy.

Tilghman Creek on the Miles River is another delightful anchorage, secluded and pretty and full of birdsong. In places its woods tumble down to the water's edge and a few scattered houses nestle among the trees. The summer fields are full of crops and there's a farmhouse with a round tower that at first sight we mistake for a church.

There are lots of small offshoots and bays to disappear into if desired but few other boats here anyway. We declare it very peaceful until a mighty roar sends us racing up on deck to find a small, four-seater seaplane hurtling towards our stern. When it is about 20 feet away it swings to starboard and pulls up onto a small beach. The pilot jumps out carrying a briefcase, but it is only when a woman and two young children come down the beach to greet him that we realise there is a house just here among the trees, and that this must be how he commutes between home and work.

I hesitate to admit what is practically heresy in a country where every home appears to have one - as do many boats – but neither of us can be bothered with the uncertainty and mess of a barbecue when there is a perfectly good stove in the galley.

Nevertheless, two nice young couples holidaying on a nearby yacht prepare a barbecue for their evening meal although all we can smell for ages is kerosene as they keep re-lighting it. And some hours later, when we go below for the night, they are still standing around looking hungry and not at all optimistic.

Our destination tomorrow morning is St Michaels, also on the Miles River, and only a little over six miles away.

30
St Michaels

We are currently reading James A Michener's sweeping, 865-page saga *Chesapeake*. The novel begins in 1583 with warring native tribes and concludes with the 1970s and the Watergate scandal. Its central themes, personified by families who settled here in Chesapeake Bay, include religion, race, poverty and industriousness, all of which remain central to American society today. Michener lived here at St Michaels while he was writing it.

It is a pretty town built around a central square instead of the usual grid system. But the first thing to strike you, if like us you dinghy in from the river, is the lighthouse on the quay. What is distinctive about it is that it is a hexagonal cottage with dormer windows and raised up on stilts. Its formal name is a screwpile lighthouse, but more often it is called 'cottage style'. It was once common in Chesapeake Bay although only one remains operational on its original site now.

The one here used to be the Hooper Strait Lighthouse until it was replaced by a modern structure in 1966 and moved to St Michaels. It has been carefully restored, is quite gorgeous and flashes throughout the night to no particular pattern that we can discern. Until, that is, we discover later that it is the letters CBMM in Morse code.

The lighthouse is part of the Chesapeake Bay Maritime Museum which is based at St Michaels and as well as artefacts contains a collection of historic buildings and boats. The town itself has some lovely old houses and a church with the most mournful carillon I've ever heard, but a very tidy graveyard. We buy fresh vegetables at the farmers' market where we are reacquainted with Greg, a trawler yacht owner we first met in Elizabeth City at the Rose Buddies' wine and cheese party.

The afternoon is spent in the cockpit enjoying another one, while around us museum staff demonstrate to their passengers the practical uses of their historic boats. An old sailing fishing boat makes several graceful passes, as does a skipjack oyster dredger.

There are also several racing log canoes, inevitably rather narrow, that have two masts from one of which they sometimes fly a spinnaker. To keep these narrow craft upright they have two boards sticking out from each side which crew members crawl out onto and act as ballast. To complete the festive atmosphere a band strikes up on shore.

Then the weather turns grey, wet and cold. Well-anchored and provisioned we decide to stay put until it improves. On one of the evenings there is a spectacular thunder storm. As always, we turn off all the electrics and wait it out. From time to time there is the crack of lightning striking a tree on the encircling banks. Then one particular bolt, probably four times thicker than the rest, connects with something with the most tremendous bang.

The next day, during a pause in the rain, we take the dinghy into St Michaels to check our emails at the library and encounter a very downcast Greg. That particularly loud bang we'd heard the previous evening was that thick bolt of lightning striking his trawler yacht. It has blown out most of his electrics, including the generator which had been running at the time, and is going to cost a small fortune in repairs.

31
Tall Ships

It is now the end of June, although it is still hard to believe this from the weather. Nevertheless, had it not kept us at St Michaels longer than we had intended we should not have witnessed something rather special. It does finally stop raining, however, the sky clears a bit and we set off for our next destination, Annapolis.

By mid-afternoon we are passing the Thomas Point Shoal Light at the entrance to the South River. Like the one at St Michaels' Maritime Museum, this lighthouse is a screwpile. It has a cupola for the light above the 1½ storey, hexagonal wooden cottage that was home to a keeper until it was automated in 1986. Unlike the one at St Michaels, however, this is a working lighthouse and equipped with a foghorn as well as a light. It is also the last one in Chesapeake still standing on its original station and one of only two in the entire country.

With its white walls, dormer windows and red roof, it seems too pretty by far. Yet at the time it was built it was the only design capable of surviving the erosion that had proved too much for its stone predecessor. The strength of the screwpile construction lay in the fact that its piles could be screwed into a soft mud or sandy bottom. This one's light was first lit in 1875.

We have just turned away from admiring it when the major treat of the day appears. Coming through the bridge from Baltimore and billowing down Chesapeake Bay is a line of tall ships. We had not known they would be here. Like the Fort Lauderdale flypast and the satellite launch at Cape Canaveral, we just happen to be in the right place at the right time.

The *Danmark*, a 252-foot Danish full-rigger, glides past with all sails set. With a draught of 17 feet, water depth is a major consideration, as it is for all these ships. They are mostly government-owned by nations around the world and used for training and education.

And while many have been updated to varying degrees, the *Danmark*, built in 1932, has retained traditional features such as steering gear without mechanical assistance, anchors raised by a capstan instead of a powered windlass and hammocks instead of bunks. When the Germans invaded Denmark during WWII she was lying off Florida. Unable to return home until 1945, she spent four years with the US Coastguard, during which time around 2,000 young Americans learned the ways of the sea.

She is followed by the *Captain Miranda*. At 210 feet, with a two-storey superstructure, she was launched in 1930 as a hydrographic survey vessel and charted the coasts and waters of Uruguay. Due to be scrapped in 1976 she was converted instead into a three-masted schooner and re-commissioned as a training ship.

Behind her the *Guayas*, a 261-foot, three-masted barque from Ecuador, carries over 15,000 square feet of sail. She was built for purpose, as a sail training ship for the Ecuadoran Navy and launched in the late 1970s.

Oosterschelde, built in 1918, is from The Netherlands and once transported clay, stone and wood. There were hundreds of these Dutch three-masted topsail schooners afloat during the early 20th century. *Oosterschelde* is the only one left and the only vessel here not government-owned. Her upkeep is paid for by private subscription and paying passengers.

These beautiful old ships are here as part of Operation Sail, or OpSail, a non-profit organisation established in 1961 by President John F Kennedy – a wartime naval officer and a keen yachtsman - under the auspices of the US Congress. Its goals are promoting goodwill and co-operation between countries, celebrating maritime history and providing training on sailing ships. Sadly President Kennedy died before the first event could take place.

OpSail invites vessels from around the world and it is sometimes referred to as 'The Tall Ships', although tall ships form only the centrepiece of the event because all sorts of sailing vessels participate, including warships. It culminates in the Parade of Ships on the Hudson River and in New York Harbour for the Independence Day celebrations on July 4, which is where the vessels currently passing our starboard beam are now heading,

This event previously took place in 1964, 1976, 1986 and 1992. So we are privileged indeed to be bobbing here, on the gentle wash of these glorious old ships on their 2000 outing as they head down Chesapeake Bay and out to sea en route for New York. The host vessel is always the *Eagle*, a 295-foot three-masted barque. Laid down in 1936 and used for training future officers of the US Coast Guard, she is the only active commissioned sailing vessel in American military service.

A question often asked is: *In today's modern navy, what is the point of sending young people out to sea under sail?* I heard it put to a senior naval officer on a radio programme around the time we embarked on our own voyage. He was responsible for the training of Royal Navy officer cadets and his answer was, 'Because it changes you.' And it does. Individuals learn that to survive you have to work as a team, to look out for each other. To be attuned to the weather and the sea and everything else around you in a way that you never can be in a large, mechanised ship. And to learn to function without state-of-the-art technology, because at some time – probably when you need it most - it is going to let you down and you need to know what to do when it does.

The last of the tall ships to pass us is the *Esmeralda*, a four-masted barquentine with graceful lines to her white hull and the second tallest and longest sailing ship in the world. It also has a dark past which makes it a questionable ambassador of goodwill at tall ship regattas and races and has inspired protests in ports around the world.

Launched as a naval training ship by the Chilean government in 1954 its function changed dramatically during the regime of General Augusto Pinochet. Reports from Amnesty International and other commissions describe the *Esmeralda* as a floating jail and torture chamber for political prisoners between 1973 and 1980.

Over a hundred people are alleged to have been incarcerated there and subjected to appalling treatment. Among them was the British priest Michael Woodward, who later died from his injuries. The controversy surrounding the ship continues because even after the restoration of democracy in Chile, no-one has ever been charged with the crimes committed on board.

32
Annapolis

Saturday morning finds us on the trots in Annapolis Harbour, swinging on a buoy in bright sunshine not far from the town. We take the dinghy early into City Dock. Early morning in summer is always the nicest time for a walk around a new town. The sun is low, the air fresh and the streets are cool and quiet. The old town is built on a low hill and Main Street rises up from the harbour.

Annapolis is named for Queen Anne, Britain's monarch from 1702 to 1714. It is the capital city of the State of Maryland and situated at the mouth of the Severn River. Many of its 17th and 18th century buildings are still here. Its State House is the oldest still in continuous use and is where the Maryland General Assembly convenes for three months each year and the elected State leadership has its offices. The two-storey brick building, in the Georgian style popular at the time, sports the largest wooden dome in the US and was constructed without nails, just wooden pegs.

Annapolis was also briefly the first capital of the new United States of America - between November 1783 and August 1784 - and is where the Continental Congress ratified the Treaty of Paris which officially ended the Revolutionary War (or War of Independence) with Britain.

It has been said of America that every few years they knock everything down and rebuild bigger and better. That may be true in some places, but in terms of their historical past Americans give every indication of going the extra mile to preserve it. They also provide the public with lots of information about historic sites and often free entry into them.

In short, great efforts are made to enthuse people – locals, out-of-towners and visitors from abroad - about their heritage. Sometimes they go a bit far for me, as regards volunteers dressing up in costume like extras on a film set, but a lot of people seem to like it. This morning we dodge milkmaids and ostlers keen to give us their perspective on olde worlde Annapolis and skitter unencumbered into the building itself.

Serendipity again. We have caught the place at its most interesting, before a scheduled restoration can varnish, gild and upholster it within an inch of its life. At present it has a delightfully well-used look. And because it is early morning there are no other visitors here yet, to clatter about with us on its bare floorboards and worn wooden stairs or stand gazing out of its tall, sash windows.

I particularly like a small, square chamber with bare wooden planks providing temporary seating in tiers on a very basic, three-sided wooden frame. I go and sit on it, to get a feel of how it might have been, when the likes of George Washington and Benjamin Franklin (the latter designed the lightning rod up on the dome) sat with their peers in this draughty room, with its modest fireplace and a large portrait of what looks like Pitt the Younger over the mantelpiece.

On Main Street, we drop off our rolls of film – paying extra for the shop's next-day service - and on our way back to our dinghy are surprised to see a man in a sharp white suit and cowboy boots on the opposite side of the road, smiling and waving his Stetson hat at the oncoming traffic.

Two people standing either side of him hold up placards saying, 'Vote for Syl!' and 'Syl for Mayor!' a candidate clearly very popular if the honking horns and cheers from passing cars is anything to go by. It is a far cry from the kind of mayoral process – formal robes and chain of office – that we are familiar with. But it looks more fun.

We will also discover that the placard on the sidewalk is standard practice in America, for all sorts of things apart from electing a new mayor. For instance, a slow day at a service station will produce a mechanic holding up a sign to oncoming traffic announcing, *Instant Lubes. Bay Free.* In fact, anything from a realtor's *Open House Day* to a furniture store's *Everything Must Go* sale will have people out on the street holding up signs. It operates in reverse, too. Disgruntled ex-workers will stand kerb-side to alert you to the fact that a particular individual or company is a very bad employer.

By the time we return to City Dock and our dinghy, downtown Annapolis has come alive. It is not for nothing, we discover, that the long channel leading from the harbour to the dockside is known as Ego Alley. This is because it is a promenade for boaters.

It is *the* place to be seen. It is putting on the style. It is where you bring your boat to be admired and it is essential that you and your guests are seen to be bronzed, relaxed and totally indifferent to any attention you might unwittingly attract from other boaters, pedestrians or diners in the dockside cafes.

Hence Ego Alley. And nobody could ever claim otherwise because there is no reason for coming down here except to be admired since all any yacht can do is motor in, turn around at City Dock with its 'Dinghies Only' notice, and motor out again.

It being a summer Saturday, it seems like everybody with a boat is out on the water and off to Ego Alley, and to get there they have to pass through the trots which they do at maximum speed. It makes for a pretty bouncy day for those of us tied up to a buoy.

Norm, our nearest neighbour, a man with an interesting past and a short fuse, gives up his attempts to compel the speedsters into obeying the no-wake regulation by the force of his lungs alone and takes to his dinghy instead. The startled boater who suddenly becomes aware of an incandescent Norm beside him tries at first to out-run him but eventually capitulates and slows down.

On Monday we wake at dawn as usual, but to the sound of chanting. Annapolis is home to the United States Naval Academy also known simply as 'Navy'. Over a period of four years it trains 4,000 midshipmen of both sexes while educating them to BSc level, and the latest first year intake (called plebes, not freshmen) are on their waterfront exercise ground at 5.45am. It is part of the rigorous Plebe Summer designed to imbue the 1300 new recruits - of whom less than a thousand are expected to graduate – with not only the spirit and discipline of the Academy but a high standard of fitness.

The effect is hypnotic, although I never do fully understand the process. Basically, the cadets, in navy blue shorts and white T-shirts, embark on their pre-breakfast callisthenics in response to their instructor. Through his megaphone, he intones in a sort of sing-song yell, 'One, two, three,' at which hundreds of midshipmen roar a number back at him. Then they perform in synch the exercise associated with that number.

So the song goes something like: 'One, two three,' followed by 1300 massed voices roaring: 'One!' and then doing the appropriate exercise.

After they have bellowed 'Three!' interspersed with calls for 'Cat Stretch!' or 'Side Stretch!' the instructor sings out, 'Four, five, six.' And all you can see for miles are shapely young bottoms in navy blue shorts. You could sell tickets.

On the other hand, what effect an amplified early-morning chant has on local property values is something only to be discovered by a delve into one of the free realtor magazines available in any supermarket doorway.

When the exercises have been completed the session concludes with a run along the waterfront and around the academy perimeter, with instructors in yellow and orange fore and aft. This culminates with the midshipmen back on the waterfront lying on their backs with their legs in the air.

Like most other institutions in America, the academy is open to the public, and you can simply wander into many of the buildings on its 300-acre site. So that's what we do. Although this openness does come as something of a shock after several decades of having your bag searched every time you enter a public building back home. But then, America has never had the IRA to worry about.

There is an excellent museum with some fascinating exhibits. And if you wish to see some gems of British maritime history this is the place to come. One of them is the model of Nelson's flagship, *Victory*, made by French prisoners of war and reputedly donated by the Royal Family for Nelson's tomb. There are also delicate bone carvings and shipbuilders' models of British warships. Although the museum's range extends beyond artefacts to the academic, such as an exploration of the background and politics of warfare.

33
Seeking Suppliers

Any publicity surrounding Annapolis usually includes the words, 'Sailing Capital of America', and an important reason for us being here is that there are a number of things we need. So we set off early down Ego Alley in the dinghy to mount a search for them. A priority is to get our two gas bottles refilled. One is empty and the other getting low and we don't want to find ourselves unable to cook or boil a kettle. We have a telephone number for the local gas bottling plant and go in search of a public phone.

We also want to do something about our electric anchor winch, which is overheating, buy a variety of spare parts, collect our mail from the Post Office, pick up our photographs and call in at the Tourist Office to find out what time the Fourth of July Parade begins tomorrow.

It turns out that our mail hasn't arrived; the gas facility says its American fittings are not compatible with British ones so it won't be able to fill our bottles and the Tourist Office won't answer any questions. The clerk just points to a magazine she hands us and keeps saying, 'It's in there. It's in there.' Only it isn't. We can't get anybody interested in fixing our anchor winch either, and the day is hot.

The Fourth of July begins like yesterday, with the call of the instructor at 5.45am, but within 15 minutes it begins to rain and all the midshipmen troop inside again. Which means that if you wake up and hear the town clock striking six but can't hear a Navy instructor's sing-song 'One, two, three,' - and the answering roar of 1300 midshipmen - you know without even opening your eyes that it is raining.

The rain stops but the day remains overcast, which keeps the heat down to an enjoyable level. We take the Jiffy water taxi to City Dock, amble up the small hill from the harbour, hang a right off Main Street and wander through the old town.

There are some lovely historic houses, with their colonial interiors, hardwood floors and generous porches. Meanwhile, Stars and Stripes flutter everywhere, among probably the ugliest collection of telegraph poles anywhere, some blackened and twisted as if they were unseasoned lumber, or the original ones, or both.

And there is blossom everywhere, tumbling from tubs and planters on the streets and cascading from the trees overhanging the brick sidewalks.

Then it's back onto Main Street to find ourselves a good kerbside spot to watch our first-ever Fourth of July Parade.

I've seen a few parades elsewhere in my time and in recent years they have always included American-style, baton-twirling cheerleaders, even in the small rural English village where we lived. Our annual summer festival seemed to attract more of them every year until finally they were arriving in hordes, bussed in from all over the country, apparently on some sort of nation-wide cheerleading schedule with a march arranged for them somewhere every summer Saturday. And apart from the colour of their uniforms they all looked eerily similar - tall, slender and cheerless. Not to mention culturally at odds with the brewery dray and shire horses, the steam traction engine, the local mountain rescue squad and the Morris dancers.

There are very few here today but the team that stands out aren't cheerleaders at all. It's a keep-fit class numbering about forty, of all ages, shapes and sizes. It even has a man lurking in the centre, bearded, middle-aged and like a number of the women a bit overweight, but all of them looking as if they are glorying in every single gyrating moment. Their slinky glide down Main Street is led by a force of nature in lycra, mostly high-stepping backwards to conduct the foot-tapping salsa rhythm her troops are following. Their enthusiasm is utterly infectious.

The colonials give us a gun salute with their muzzleloaders; there are lots of people in colonial uniforms including some from the Navy, Redcoats drumming, women in bodices, aprons and caps and a band in T-shirts and Stetsons including a number of very earnest-looking children determined to get it right. Particularly popular, though, are the local animal shelter's two representatives, an elderly Labrador-cross and a beagle. Both are wearing their corporate neckerchiefs and shyly acknowledge the cheering crowd, while the woman driving the van beside them leans out of the window shouting hopefully over the mayhem to a volunteer, 'Hand out the *Adopt a Stray* leaflets!'

Something they have here that we never had at our annual village fete is a political element. In an open-topped car sits the town's mayoral candidate we saw working the street on Saturday, waving to the crowd with his 'Vote for Syl' placards propped up on the back seat.

Something absent here is alcohol. At home the local pubs (and there were quite a few of them) stayed open throughout festival day and the last one we went to, before we sailed away, attracted an unusual amount of drunken youths from outside the village who spoiled the atmosphere and made the cheerleaders even more glum then ever by shouting insults at them.

We are back on board *Voyager* by the time the fireworks begin. When we had been told that they would be coming from a barge anchored in the harbour we hadn't realized that it would be just off our stern. It is far enough away not to shed burning fragments over our decks, but close enough to fill our horizon with light, colour and pattern in the most spectacular display. Talk about a ringside seat! We are deaf for days.

During the course of the day a large number of boats had gathered in the anchorage near the harbour entrance and their anchor lights have glimmered softly in the darkness throughout the evening. Now, with the fireworks over, they putter sedately towards home in flickering skeins of light - some to their moorings outside the harbour, others back to anchor in Spa Creek - their navigation lights vanishing as they pass beyond the harbour entrance or under Spa Creek Bridge, like candles being snuffed out one by one.

David sets off at eight next morning for the Mall (which he has to remember to pronounce *mawl* when asking directions or risk confusing people) to get a TV, a phone, our photographs, our post, some food, and dispose of our domestic refuse. He manages the last-mentioned quite quickly but after that his day goes downhill.

In the meantime I tune into a local radio station to learn a little of our new surroundings while I do something about the bathroom. The first item is that Delaware, a neighbouring State, has enacted legislation outlawing animal fighting and the use of cat and dog fur in manufactured products. America may be one of the most advanced nations in the world but not in everything, apparently. Almost as surprising is the advertisement that follows.

Something which America may not have invented, but has raised to the level of an art form, is shopping. Accordingly, every event in the national calendar is seen as a retailing opportunity and extended to the nth degree. Thus Memorial Day, which we celebrated along with other boaters on the last Monday in May, became the three-day Memorial Day Weekend. Even this is insufficient for a truly aspiring marketing team, however, and the airwaves and billboards were filled with Memorial Day Week Sales. But the radio advertisement now being broadcast for a department store - warning listeners not to miss out *on the fifth and final week of our Memorial Day Weekend Month Sale* - takes the process to a whole new level. Not least because all those people currently enjoying the Fourth of July holiday will be available to take advantage of the Memorial Day bargains still on offer.

Meanwhile I've embarked on some serious polishing. Like the rest of our boat, the bathroom is moulded from fibreglass. After a time its gelcoat does not respond fully to a standard bathroom cleaner. Soap residue and calcium deposits from the water form a patina that makes surfaces dull. The answer is to give them a thorough going over with the same kind of marine polish you use on the topsides and decks and with a generous amount of elbow grease a sink that had looked in need of replacing will emerge like new.

The bath is a deep triangular corner one with a moulded seat, which is ideal for a boat because you can sit and shower in safety even with jet skiers doing wheelies round your hull. Its depth also contains the water better than a shower tray. The only problem is that to polish it you have to stand in it, which means that the bottoms of your feet end up getting polished as well. And by the time I've finished I can't move without slipping, even on the non-slip wooden grating. And having polished the washbasin, the floor, the walls and the loo, the entire room is now a death trap.

A telephone, David reports wearily on his return, appears to be an insuperable problem because we don't have a US address. Anything remotely connected with credit in this country is difficult for people like us and a phone is considered credit because you will run up a bill for calls. So what they do is take an $800 bond off people against future calls. However, we can't buy a phone even if we pay this bond because we don't have a credit rating. You only have a credit rating if you owe money, or have owed it in the past, and have, or are, paying it back at the appropriate rate. 'But I don't owe any money,' David had explained, 'anywhere.' This was considered deeply suspicious and he wasn't allowed to buy a phone.

Our photos aren't ready, despite our paying for the 'day-after delivery option' five days ago, and our post still hasn't arrived. David had also assumed there would be food at the mall but failed to find any. Some towns and cities will have a small supermarket in the town centre or shopping mall – a sort of mini-market. But the Annapolis food store is miles out of town. Accordingly, we are having pilchards for tea, this being the most interesting tin currently gracing our depleted larder.

But David rarely returns empty-handed and we now have a $60, black-and-white, 5-inch screen, portable TV. It is over a year since we last watched a television programme. The first one we manage to tune into is *Last of the Summer Wine* in which Compo does Maurice Chevalier impersonations on a northern TV show whose presenter is a boyish Gordon Kaye, the future middle-aged cafe owner from *'Allo, Allo'* - so that's a clue to how old it is.

In fact, squint up your eyes a bit and you enter a time warp of 1950s small-screen black-and-white televisions and historic programming. Classic British TV programmes, we will discover, are a staple of a number of America's many channels, from *Monty Python* and *Benny Hill* to *As Time Goes By*. After watching a few of them again after all these years I find myself wondering if somewhere, out there in the ether, the potter's wheel is still circling, along with Lord Reith's code on sex, violence and bad language in broadcasting.

David's next sortie ashore is another attempt to find someone to fill our propane gas bottles. Trying to explain over a public telephone, to someone who finds your English accent a bit difficult anyway, that they *can* fill our bottles using our own connector hose, while noisily pumping in coins which don't quite fit the slot, is proving fruitless. They need to see the hose. So, given his orienteering training on the city's bus system yesterday, off he goes.

His first visit is to the bottling plant he contacted from the phone box last week and who said our fitting was incompatible. Looking at our spare connector hose now the man behind the counter says they could have done it for us last week after all. Unfortunately they are now in the process of moving premises, and getting their tank installed in the new place could take anything up to three weeks.

He then tries a service station which someone tells him also sells propane. The girl on duty says she can't fill them herself but if he comes again tomorrow morning the manager will be in and she may be able to do it. He gives up on gas and goes in search of charts and a cruising guide for the next stage of our journey. His trip inland has taken four buses with some long waits in between and he does not return until 5.30pm. I greet him with the news that the fridge has stopped working. The only upside is that not having yet visited a supermarket there is little in it to spoil anyway.

David will have to go ashore again tomorrow and telephone a boat refrigeration company. On small Caribbean islands local services tended to cluster around the main harbour. You would dinghy ashore from the anchorage and what you needed was usually to be found near where you tied up. And, with so many foreign cruisers, the islands were used to dealing with lots of different types of boats. In Annapolis they are only used to dealing with American ones. Also, the majority of yachtsmen here are locals, or they commute to their boats from nearby cities like Washington and Baltimore.

Either way, they have a car. So a supplier on an industrial site miles away on the far side of town is not a problem. At present the days are peaking at around 100°F. An aluminium dinghy gets hot. A public telephone box is like stepping into an oven. David decides we can no longer function without a mobile telephone. But how to get one without an address?

The answer comes in the form of a local yachtsman. Overhearing our plight he offers to receive our invoices, which are only confirmation anyway since payment will be made by direct debit through our bank. David sets off for City Dock next morning in the dinghy and takes a bus to the telephone store.

He returns quite a long time later with some food but also to look for a bank statement from our US bank, because the phone store says it will accept this as a credit rating. I tell him the fridge has now fully defrosted and although I have fired up the starboard engine again it will not re-chill.

'I'll see to it as soon as I get the phone,' he says. Then it's back into the dinghy to City Dock, up the hill to the bus station, nearly an hour's wait for a bus because he's just missed one, a long bus ride, then a walk to the telephone store where he hands over our bank statement.

'Thank you,' says the clerk. 'And I'll want to see your passport.' With the prospect of another three hours spent catching buses, dinghying through the harbour and traipsing up hills in 100-degree heat David takes the only sensible option. He throws a tantrum on the sales floor and they let him buy a phone.

When he calls the marine refrigeration firm a man says he will come out either tomorrow afternoon or Monday, and he will ring tomorrow morning to confirm which. But whatever happens, we will have the fridge working by Monday night.

With no confirmation from the fridge company forthcoming, David telephones again on Monday. Someone will be coming out tomorrow, he is told, but they will ring tomorrow to confirm.

Life without a fridge in these temperatures is difficult. You can't just pop round the corner for the day's meal when you are a dinghy ride and a bus journey from a grocery store. And you crave a cold drink.

Another call to the company elicits the same response as yesterday: *Someone will call you tomorrow to confirm they are coming.*

In a mood of desperation I say, 'Why don't we try it again. Just in case. You never know.'

Instead of the usual gas/batteries/mains-electricity fridge, ours is powered by running the starboard engine for around 50 minutes a day. It is ideal for a boat without access to mains electricity most of the time and if you are motor-sailing you get a cold fridge automatically as part of your journey.

David turns the engine on without much confidence but within minutes it is apparent that the refrigerator plate is beginning to chill. On reflection he thinks the failure may have been caused by a tall drinks carton that had been stored directly under the valve and which had caused the valve to freeze up. With the carton gone, the valve has defrosted and begun functioning again. Whatever the reason, the outcome is fortunate because the refrigerator company never does call back.

34
The Locals

Although one might want to question the town's claim to be The Sailing Capital of America in terms of boat supplies – for this foreign yacht at least - you can't fault the people running the public services. They are a delight. Annapolis runs a free bus service and the drivers are wonderful. They see everyone on and off the vehicle without rush. There is a large sign saying not to leave your seat before the bus stops, which is nice, because it tells you unequivocally that the driver will not lurch away before you can stagger to the exit with all your shopping bags and send you crashing down the aisle into the windscreen.

The road works in the middle of town have interrupted the bus schedules and on one occasion the bus we want is 45 minutes overdue. Before we start walking I go over and ask the driver of a newly-arrived Yellow if by any chance a Brown B is behind her. She asks where we want to go and then says, 'Get on this one and I'll put you on the right one.' She then phones ahead to say we are coming and when we reach the transfer point she directs us to a Red which sets off immediately we board. We hop straight off the Red and into the public library to do our emails. *Eaton Square, my man, and quick about it!*

The cashiers in the supermarket and those collecting shopping carts (no coins needed, by the way) all smile and speak nicely to each other as well as to you. I still treasure the memory of one I once shopped at, where a door flew outwards, scattering me and a number of other shoppers as half a dozen stony-faced staff swept en mass out of Customer Service and fanned across the store, totally ignoring their customers and each other.

The lady in the launderette, thin as a whippet, sweeping and clearing fluff from the dryers, and with a face that seems to smile as a natural state, is quite one of the nicest people I have ever met. As is Henry, one of her patrons. He asks if we ever go to see the Queen and is concerned that while his father was 95 when he died and his mother in her mid-eighties, average life expectancy now is only 70. He ascribes much of the problem to the food: too much sugar, he says, and just ... *too much.* 'All you-can-eat menus encourage greed.'

Accessing our emails at the public library is not only free but cheerfully provided. It isn't always so in American towns. In one of them the librarian kept padding back and forth looking over our shoulders in case we were doing something inappropriate. Most have charged so far, one requiring a $25 temporary membership fee and holding my driver's licence as collateral. I've no idea what she thought I was going to do.

Private citizens are also very hospitable. A local man we run into several times ashore invites us home to dinner with his family. He picks us up at City Dock. At the end of the evening he hands us his car keys to get back to our dinghy. 'I'll pick up the car tomorrow,' he says. As David negotiates unlit, heavily-wooded back roads in an unfamiliar car we pray we find the harbour before the Highway Patrol finds us - driving without insurance papers or ID, and with no way of explaining who gave us the car or where he lives, because we don't know.

And with our fridge functional again even Norm's gentler side reveals itself when he volunteers the use of his car for a big supermarket shop-up. But in case he should be suspected of going soft he growls, 'One time only!' as he tosses over the keys.

Our post finally arrives at the post office as do the photographs at the photo shop, where David is given a refund on their next-day delivery charge because they are a week late. We also have a full refrigerator and food cupboards, spare parts, a mobile phone and a TV. And since the weekend is approaching, with its inevitable tidal wave from Ego Alley and Norm's blood pressure at dangerously high levels, we are ready to move on.

We need a bit of still water for a couple of days and nearby Whitehall Bay is just the place. The duck hide at its entrance has a sheepish-looking osprey in a ramshackle nest on top of it, but at least the chicks will be fledged before the duck shooting season begins.

The weekend produces two heavily overcast, pleasantly cool days, ideal for cleaning the boat, with David in the dinghy buffing away a diesel slick along the waterline and the brown peaty residue of the ICW from *Voyager*'s bows. The ICW is famous for leaving boats with a characteristic brown stain on their bows, known from its downward curve as 'the ICW moustache'. Meanwhile I go to work on the cockpit and decks.

We have to take a rest after Sunday lunch. All the stress is concentrated in the right elbow and the small of the back, with neither functioning properly and very painful. If only you could spread the ache around a wider area. But after the heat and bustle of Annapolis, the perfect peace of a shady Sunday afternoon in this wide, deserted bay is bliss.

35
Back On Chesapeake

Half an hour after leaving Whitehall Bay next day we reach the Chesapeake Bay Bridge which is a little short of four and a half miles long (or wide if, like us, you're travelling under it). Just as the ungainly camel is said to have been designed by a committee, this bridge resembles something where a number of individuals were asked to design one section of it each and who then handed over their drawings to the builder without any consultation with their fellow-designers.

No two sections seem to have the same type of stanchions or spans, not even the two ends which one feels should, aesthetically speaking, have been identical. A similar effect might be achieved by buying up second-hand bridges and bolting them together. What we don't realize, in the gauzy light of an overcast morning, is that some of the effect is caused by there being *two* spans – the original from 1952 and the second built twenty years later – one close behind the other.

When you reach it you discover its steel roadway. Passing underneath it you look up at the underside of vehicle chasses roaring overhead, their wheels on the metal grid producing an unbroken howl that jolts you to your feet as you suddenly hit a wall of sound.

It is also, we discover later, a very scary bridge to drive over – so much so that some people pay professionals to drive them and their cars over it. Aspects which produce anxiety in drivers apparently include a dogleg curve, a steep incline, the swoop between two suspension spans and a cantilever section resembling a claustrophobic tunnel.

From the bridge, as the crow flies, it is just over four miles to the mouth of the Chester River but you have to go an extra two-and-a-half miles north round the Love Point Light to avoid shallow water. After you've turned back on yourself, you enter a wide river estuary with a navigable channel marked with buoys.

After a few miles the river divides into four cruisable branches. One of them is still the Chester River, only now it is much narrower, shallow and full of bends, and to follow the buoys you find yourself lurching from bank to bank. This is because, as the river runs downstream into Chesapeake Bay, it scours the outside of the numerous bends, which is where the deeper water that boats need is to be found.

The Chester River is around 43 miles long and a major tributary of Chesapeake Bay. It has a beautiful shoreline of fields and barns, woodland and rolling countryside; and also mansions and estates thanks to an early 18th century shipping boom here which created a wealthy merchant class.

Chestertown lies at its navigable head, 26 miles upstream. It was founded in 1706 but came into its own when it was named one of Maryland's six Royal Ports of Entry - a place where merchandise was received, duties paid and customs and navigation laws enforced. This precipitated the shipping boom that produced not only the country estates we passed on the way up here, but the 18th century mansions and town houses we now admire gracing its waterfront.

It is a very pretty town and one that draws deeply on its past as a way of attracting tourists. An annual event is the Chestertown Tea Party Festival which local tradition says occurred in 1774 when a cargo of tea was thrown into the Chester River in protest at British excise duties, although there doesn't appear to be any actual evidence that it ever happened. *Like Boston*, someone tells us. *Lots of little shops put up along the street you can go inside. Nice.*

Back on *Voyager* the real drama of the day begins. The thing David always hoped he would never have to do - unblock the toilet. Brevity is essential here, but the poor man goes into that hellhole at around 3pm and does not finally emerge until two hours later. All that must be done has to be done crouching into a small cupboard 19 inches high and 7 inches wide. Add heat and bad air and men have gone stark mad. He is uncomplaining as always.

Afterwards I give him a couple of cold beers in the cockpit while he cools a little. He has a shower. He sits out in the cockpit, silently, for a long time. I feed him. He goes to bed. We just hope that no curious dumpster-diver decides to untie the plastic bag we deposit in the bin on the quay before we leave.

Sunrise is bright red and after that it becomes a pale blue, sparkling morning. The sunlight glints off the water like candlelight off crystal, and blazes off the davits and brightwork. Somewhere osprey are cheep-cheeping. We meander back down the Chester River and once out into the Chesapeake Bay head for Rock Hall.

On the way we stop for fuel, but especially water as we are well down our second tank. It is a pretty place, just becoming a marina. Piles driven into water that still laps cleanly up a small sandy beach bordered by bright green grass and two glorious, blossom-laden trees. Not yet established, with sour, diesel-stained water and green slimy piles. A youth, so typical of small American towns, leaves a half-built pontoon to come over and serve us. Open, guileless.

'We're still building,' he says, by way of apology for the incomplete nature of the place. 'But we're gettin' there.' And as he talks, unaffected, amiable, those young faces on a Washington memorial come unbidden to mind. Boys like this one, shipped off to a world so unexpected, so inexplicable. Irrationally, I want to throw my arms around him.

Instead I say, 'Thank you,' as he hands me the water hose. For his courtesy. His innocence. His unconscious sweetness.

'Take all the time you need,' he says, leaving us to fill our embarrassingly slow-filling water tanks. Going off in the sweat-inducing heat, wiping his face with the edge of his T-shirt, to lie on his stomach on the unfinished pontoon with his arms reaching down to the water's edge, holding a plank while an older man hammers it into place.

36
Rock Hall

Rock Hall Harbour is a semi-circle of marinas, boatyards and waterside crab restaurants around a bay protected by two breakwaters. Our purpose in coming here is to get our propane gas bottles filled. The situation is now critical. According to our cruising guide there is only one marina that keeps it and warns that the water outside the narrow channel leading to it is very shallow.

I warn David of something in the water and he diverts slightly to avoid it in case it is a submerged fishing buoy. It turns out to be a dead fish but in avoiding it we run aground on a mud bank. The tide charts tell us that we are two hours after high tide and since there is only a 1-foot tide here we will not be able to get off until 10pm tonight, if at all.

David takes our dinghy the few yards to the marina and returns in a workboat with a man called Jay. There used to be a marker, he says, but a yacht wrote it off some time ago and the Coast Guard hasn't got around to replacing it yet. The workboat pulls fore and aft and, despite our port engine refusing to start, after a bit of a struggle we slide off the mud bank.

We finally tie up to the marina's fuel dock and present our gas bottles only to find they no longer refill them here. However, this is small town America. A man sets off in a truck with both our bottles. He returns soon after to say that the bottling plant operator has never seen an English bottle, doesn't understand 'kilowatts' and is not happy, but with a little encouragement by way of explanation he will probably oblige.

He gives David the keys to the truck and directions to the bottling plant. The plant operator is a big countryman who is mollified by a conversion from kilograms to pounds, and by being allowed to fill the bottles to only 27lbs instead of 28. The only difference is between metric and imperial measurement. The bottle and connector are exactly the same. David returns with two full gas bottles.

Our next job is to get the port engine working. It needs a new solenoid. David rings a firm from the marina. They can see one on their computer, they say, but can't locate it in their stock room. They mount a search but 45 minutes later call back to say they still can't find it. A man called Bob takes David in his Volvo to find one.

Fitting it is delayed briefly while Jay takes out the workboat to prise another yacht off the same mud bank we grounded on. When he comes aboard *Voyager* he is accompanied by JJ (Jay Junior) an enormous, grey Burmese cat, clipped short except for a whisk on the end of his tail which flicks constantly. We assume this is the operative referred to in the notice on the marina window saying *Beware: Attack Trained Cat*. He has wonderful wide yellow eyes and after a careful inspection of us makes himself completely at home in the saloon, tail flicking like a metronome, while Jay installs the new solenoid.

Meanwhile, I take our washing to the laundry room. This is quite the prettiest marina I've ever been in. All the facilities, including the shower room and lavatories, are not only sumptuous but have beautifully-curtained windows. The laundry is located in The Carriage House, a two-storey wooden building. The lending library upstairs has a balcony with rocking chairs and a delightful view.

We decide to stay the night. We also buy two round wooden tokens for tomorrow's 8.20am trolley. This is a small, decorative, single-decker bus, very popular in tourist areas and reminiscent of the old-fashioned, square-cornered trolleybus of yore but with big windows and brass handrails.

During the night, from the bars and restaurants across the bay come the strains of 1960s hits, muted by distance into pleasurable reminiscence as we drift off to sleep.

There is a lovely sunrise. The fishermen are going out and two geese on the fish dock serenade the new day: first one goose lifts its head and gives a honk and then the other. A huge grey heron flies over and they break off from their duet to honk aggressively at it. The heron, usually such a quiet bird, is so incensed it barks ferociously back at them.

Sometimes, on these glorious warm summer mornings we're up and breakfasted so early we have mid-morning coffee around 8am. Like this morning. After which we present ourselves at the trolley's stopping place opposite our pontoon and wait. And wait. As 9am approaches we hail a passing yachtswoman. She smiles knowingly.

'He'll *be* here,' she is sure of that. The question left hanging is *When*? She can't be specific because last night was karaoke night at one of the crab houses across the bay. 'He may be a little late,' she says. 'But he'll *definitely* be here.' Both the sun and the temperature are rising. 'There's always bicycles,' she offers hopefully.

And so there are, free on request from the boatshed and the means of a delightful ride into the small town of Rock Hall. If the marina is picture perfect, with its beautifully maintained wooden buildings and luxuriant flower beds, the road leading towards town is no less so. Initially it is hedged by maize, well above head height, stately and lush. After that, mown grass and neat clapboard houses.

Fortunately for me the road is relatively flat and I don't have the ignominy of having to get off my bike and push it up any hills. The little town has a nice atmosphere, a cafe at the crossroads and the post office we need. Back at the marina we are returning the bicycles to the boat yard just as the trolley pulls up.

37
Still Pond

On the journey to Still Pond Creek, a couple of miles south of the Sassafras River, it is so hot I have to put on shoes as it is too painful to step out on the open deck barefoot. And it being Saturday there are a lot of pleasure craft about.

The cruising guide says that the outer basin of Still Pond gets crowded and boisterous at weekends but that the creek running into it is tranquil. So we go in there. And it is. It is also very shallow at this state of the tide, especially just where you enter, and we end up hugging the bank to stay afloat.

The weather, changeable as ever, then threatens rain for hours, with the sky even turning vaguely orange in the distance - like a Chesapeake Duster, with navy blue cloud overhead - but after three drops on the canopy, nothing happens. Except for the barn swallows, with their reddish lower face and throat, and beaks too wide for their faces, giving them a grim, rather indignant expression full-face but a little button beak in profile.

They come in groups and settle on the starboard bow rail. There, with the suppleness of ballet dancers at the bar, they embark on a rigorous grooming routine. Heads disappear over shoulders and beaks rootle about in downy chests. A wing is opened and spread like a fan, the head disappearing into it so that a busy beak can scissor its way through the flight feathers. Buffed and coiffed and stripped of parasites, as one group leaves another settles in.

Sunday morning we take a wander down the creek in the dinghy. You rather expect a creek to be narrow, whereas this one is as wide as some rivers we've been on. There are herons everywhere - among the reeds, on tree branches, and standing in natural camouflage among upturned tree roots that are the same shape, size and colour as themselves.

The banks provide endless variety: wild flowers, bull rushes, a piece of driftwood on a tiny beach, a great many trees and a partially-hidden clearing with a hint of garden furniture darkly discerned. The occasional small jetty, a solitary wooden bench half-hidden among trees, a house tucked away on top of the heavily wooded banks, but barely visible. Letting you feel you have the creek all to yourselves. Secret. Tranquil.

Early evening a heron slowly patrols its territory in the shallow water of the shore opposite *Voyager*. Two bald eagles land a short distance away and begin taking it in turns to pick over a large fish on the narrow bank. A third bald eagle lands. This latest is a youngster, brown speckled, without the white head and tail. The two adults guard it while it straddles the corpse with its fat furry legs and bright yellow feet, and eats voraciously.

The heron, refusing to be displaced from its own turf, has now stopped only a few feet away. The young eagle takes a run at it and roars. The heron raises its wings and roars back, but refuses to budge an inch. The young eagle goes back to eating. Meanwhile, two turkey vultures have begun circling overhead.

The young eagle gives off eating after a while and walks into the water near the heron for a drink. It returns to eat again, but is driven away by one of the adult eagles which has resumed its place at the fish. The heron is now patrolling slowly along the shoreline again, at one stage ignoring the young eagle stalking along behind it like a mocking schoolboy.

Quite suddenly there are *three* adult bald eagles, plus the youngster, while the two turkey vultures have landed and are standing, waiting their turn. The heron continues to slowly patrol his territory and is not going to leave for anybody.

It is a large fish and when the eagles fall back, the vultures set to. Then, amazingly, the heron strolls up out of the water, steps in between the two startled vultures, takes a bite out of the fish, savours it, and then saunters back to the water's edge where it resumes its patrol.

After about an hour all have had their fill and gone and the heron has its territory to itself again. It shows no further interest in the dead fish, preferring to catch its own live ones.

38
Chesapeake & Delaware Canal

When we start up the engines next morning we find that our depth gauge isn't working. As we set off, an extraordinary butterfly wafts across our cockpit, black & white stripes, with long tail pieces, and wider than my hand. When I look it up later, the book says it is a Zebra Swallowtail, not an imaginative name perhaps but describing it perfectly.

The depth gauge finally wobbles into life as we reach the narrow bend at the entrance to the creek and is showing something over 15 feet when we run aground. On the bank opposite ten turkey vultures are gathered around another fish. A heron lands and stalks among them. Herons really like to mix it with vultures although it was noticeable that the doughty river warden of yesterday did not take any liberties with adult bald eagles.

David revs the engines like mad for a bit, to try and pull us off the mud, but despite my urging will not steer over to the right. Instead he consults the tide chart - one hour to go to low tide, so we'll need three hours more to get enough water under us again.

Then we have an argument because I insist he should have aimed to the right and he says he couldn't because he would have hit another shoal and I say rubbish, that's the channel. With gritted teeth we lower the dinghy.

David steers while I measure the depth around *Voyager* with the boathook, and we argue some more because over on the right it is deep but he won't accept that he was wrong and alters what he had said at the time and I tell him he has changed the facts as usual and he says the depth gauge confused the hell out of him and I ask why keep going on about a fallible bit of plastic when all I've asked him to do is at least try something I am sure about, and the vultures glower at us and the heron walks off in disgust. We climb back onto *Voyager*, start her up, rev the engines, steer to the right and in a couple of minutes we're on our way.

We are now leaving Chesapeake Bay and continuing our journey north via the Chesapeake & Delaware Canal which turns out to be extremely pretty: dense woodland in places and interspersed with brightly-painted clapboard houses. The canal was dug to join Chesapeake Bay and Delaware Bay, and is the quickest way north. The alternative is to go all the way back down Chesapeake Bay again and out to sea.

About a quarter of the way along the canal there is a village called Chesapeake City with a small harbour where transients like us can tie up or anchor. We expect to anchor, as its free dock will undoubtedly be full at the end of July. But it has only a small pleasure boat on it, so we tie up and take a wander round the town.

Formerly known as The Village of Bohemia, Chesapeake City is a small village of attractive 19th century houses, many of them now guest houses and antique shops. In 1824 it was the hub of the 14-mile long Chesapeake & Delaware Canal's construction. Most of the homes that were built between 1830 and 1860 still stand today. One of them, built around 1854 in Georgian Federal style, is The Blue Max Inn, once occupied by Jack Hunter, author of *The Blue Max* a best-selling novel about WWI fliers. The inn is girded with porches, two storeys high, around front and sides and probably the back as well if we could but see.

Back on the dock we are joined by a Dutchman, Laurens, and his young son from Baltimore in their 30-foot sloop *Wave Dancer*. They have been on a month-long family cruise, the wife and daughter having flown home leaving them to return the boat. The son confides that sailing with two, rather than four, is much nicer. Laurens tells us about Maine. *Beautiful, foggy, and plentiful lobster – four or five dollars off the boats - and you can collect your own mussels off the rocks as Americans don't care for them.*

As we talk a large motor yacht with 'Just Married' on the side skitters into the harbour sideways, revving and roaring and creating a terrific wash. It is shortly followed by a second motor yacht which does something similar.

The entrance to this little harbour can be treacherous due to the strong current in the canal which, as you make the turn into the harbour, carries you sideways towards the entrance wall. So you have to take it at a faster speed than you would like for such a small harbour, and then be ready to throttle back as soon as you are free of the current's grip.

We have dinner on the dock of the marina next door. A man steps ashore from the latest arrival – a very large power boat – and hands the marina manager a vast array of thick yellow cables and connectors. There's enough to supply the QEII and when we leave, thirty minutes later, they are still trying to work out which does what.

After a walk around town under a spectacular, old-gold, flaring sunset, we retire for a game of chess before bed. It rains all night long.

We go up on deck early next morning into a cold, grey, drizzle and wave off father and son on *Wave Dancer*, leaving for home in their oilies and with a final injunction from Laurens to get to Maine. Everybody raves about Maine. Then we go back to bed for a bit as we need the tide to turn before we head east.

At 10am it still feels like winter.

'Remind me,' says David. 'Is this global warming or the start of the New Ice Age?'

Noon is the optimum time for us to leave but it is still raining and we decide to remain another day. But after lunch the sky seems to be clearing so we change our minds again and go. There is less than a foot of water under our keel as we leave and we realise that the yacht which has been 'hovering' just inside the harbour entrance for some time is actually aground.

About an hour into our journey we pass through the ConRail Bridge, always left open unless a train is due. According to one of our pilot books this system failed tragically in January 1862 when, during a blizzard, the guard failed to see that the light was against him and the engine plunged into the canal with 13 empty wagons and a passenger coach piling in on top of it. The guard managed to jump clear but the engineer and the fireman perished.

NEW JERSEY

39

Delaware Bay

Our cruising guides warn sailors to take Delaware Bay seriously because of strong currents and even stronger winds. This bay is, in fact, an enormous estuary and part of its challenging nature comes from the fact that the Delaware River's strong current flows down it from the north, while Atlantic tides push up it from the south. Meanwhile, a constant flow of cargo ships pass between the ocean and the busy deep-water ports of Philadelphia and Wilmington.

From the Chesapeake & Delaware Canal where we join it, down to Cape May peninsular where it enters the ocean, the Delaware Bay is 60 miles long and 25 miles across at its widest point. The towns on the New Jersey side grew up around oystering, using sailing vessels of the kind we saw taking tourists for a spin at St Michaels. All gone from here now, of course. But so have the oysters. After WWII power dredgers rapidly depleted stocks, followed in 1957 by the mysterious MSX disease which destroyed the beds.

Visibility is poor, there are a lot of big commercial ships that we need to avoid, and by mid-day we have only another two hours of favourable tide which is not long enough to get us to Cape May. So we decide to anchor up until tomorrow and head for the Cohansey River, our first stop in New Jersey. Negotiating its entrance we have only 8inches of water under our keel. As well as shallow it is probably the most winding river we have ever encountered. As it twists and turns through the marshes, in places it all but meets itself coming back.

It is also a river where Captain Kidd is alleged to have buried some of his treasure. Mind you, William 'Captain' Kidd is alleged to have buried treasure as far afield as Canada, the Caribbean, Japan and Vietnam. What with all that long-distance sailing, the effort needed to provision a boat for a hungry and thirsty crew, acquiring treasure in the first place and then having to bury it to retain it, you wonder when he ever got to enjoy any of it. Or even *if*. What is known for sure is that after being held in appalling conditions in London he was hanged aged 46 and then displayed in chains over the River Thames as a deterrent to other would-be pirates.

This is not a bad anchorage. There is no wind to disturb the water although the current is strong enough to make a bow wave at the height of the tide. And it is very quiet, just a couple of other boats; until the horseflies move in. Lots of them, with their shiny, almost luminous green heads. You can't brush them off as they have their fangs stuck into you, sucking blood. You have to hit them really hard to dislodge them, but they simply get up and start coming at you again. It can take two or three determined thumps with the swatter against a hard surface to finish them off. Even then, they sometimes recover and come crawling back for more. We go inside, screen every hatch, close the companionway doors, kill anything that moves that isn't us and remain inside staring out. Like a scene from *Sean of the Dead*, only smaller.

As if spending a muggy night sealed indoors against blood-sucking creatures isn't enough, something peculiar seems to be happening to *Voyager*. We twist and turn in incomprehensible ways in the pitch darkness, go to bed and get up again because what we can see from our bed in terms of two other anchor lights makes no sense at all and we fear we must be dragging.

The prospect of re-anchoring is appalling. Fortunately, before we render up our flesh to the local bug population David realizes that we are actually lying sideways across the river. The wind has come up and is driving our three boats in one direction while the current is sending us in another. The reason we are at odds with one another is that our different types of hull are responding differently to the forces pushing against them.

Our two neighbours leave early next morning, going north. Our way is south and we need to wait for the tide to turn. The marsh grass looks very lush and is a wonderful green but a rather nasty smell keeps wafting off it, like something rotting. It is our first encounter with marsh gas.

Once out of the Cohansey River we set a course for the Ship John Shoal Light and then turn down the bay past Joe Flogger Shoal, running parallel with the ship channel. Some huge barges pass from both directions. One of them heading for the sea is stacked with what seems an enormous amount of containers and looks particularly intimidating. We have anchored off smaller islands.

All these vessels are formidable at close quarters anyway, because of their size, and the reason that we are staying out of the ship channel itself. Open dry cargo barges are 200 feet long and carry 1,500 tons. Inland liquid tank barges are 300 feet long and carry a million gallons.

When the water has settled down again we become aware of a graceful movement beside us. It turns out to be a family of stingrays, light brown in colour: two adults, one medium-sized and an infant. The adults break the surface of the water rhythmically and delicately, with just the tips of their wings meeting briefly over their heads.

Further down the bay David suggests that we take the Cape May Canal short cut which will save us time going round the shoals at the tip of the peninsula. The only problem is a 55-foot fixed bridge – ten feet lower than standard - leaving us with only a two-foot clearance at low tide and cutting things a bit fine.

I agree that we should take the canal route, but suspect I am not going to enjoy it.

40

Cape May

Britain was the reason the Cape May Canal was built. As World War II progressed Britain could no longer grow enough food or manufacture sufficient munitions to supply its own populace and its troops around the globe. Canadian, and later American, supplies were vital for Britain to survive the war and were transported by convoys of merchant ships. In the North Atlantic, one of the departure points for these convoys was Cape May.

Unfortunately, the ships soon became a target for German U-boats waiting off the peninsula at the mouth of Delaware Bay. The loss of lives, shipping and vital supplies was devastating. In 1942 the American response was to have its Army Corps of Engineers dredge the three-mile long Cape May Canal. This enabled ships to exit through the Cape May Inlet and get into open water quickly, instead of via the exposed Cape May Point whose sand banks and shoals made it difficult for the ships to take evasive action from German torpedoes.

The lower-than-usual fixed bridge which we now have to negotiate is roughly half-way down this canal. The plan had been to arrive at low tide, giving us maximum clearance for *Voyager*'s mast. Unfortunately we get there about an hour after low tide, leaving our 55-foot clearance reduced and David less confident than he was.

To make matters worse, now that he has studied the chart he finds that there are three bridges to get through, not one as shown in the cruising guide, including a swing bridge which is open 95% of the time and only closed when a train is due. We see the first bridge and it looks very low. To make matters worse the swing bridge just behind it is closed, causing traffic to back up in the canal and further delay on a rising tide. You always know it is time to worry when people gather on the banks to watch your progress. Parents begin pointing out the top of our mast to their children.

Eventually a one-carriage train goes through and the swing bridge opens. The canal traffic clears in a rush making a lot of wash. We bounce up and down in it, which is bad for the nerves when your mast is in imminent danger of connecting with something solid, but after the wash calms down we tentatively approach the first bridge.

The crew on a following boat, seeing our hesitation and with possibly a better view of our chances than we have, give us the thumbs-up and we decide to go for it.

As we clear the bridge with relief, a sports fishing boat comes roaring towards the swing bridge from the other direction, as it has precedence with the tide behind it. We grind to a halt in the small space between the two bridges to let it through, but then its skipper realizes our predicament, stops for us and circles in the channel to wait.

After we pass under the final bridge the boat which had been following, and had waved us through, comes alongside.

'How much clearance did we have in the end?' I ask one of the crew.
He holds his palms about nine inches apart.

Having scraped under the bridge our next priority is not to run aground in the very shallow waters of Cape May Harbour. We find enough water to remain afloat in, when the tide goes out, off the Coastguard station and drop our hook.

A yacht under sail glides past and its skipper calls out a warning that this harbour is rather rolly. How right he is. The cause is boats roaring through, some with engines up to 1400hp (*Voyager*'s two combined total 54) which makes them capable of very high speeds.

In a gentler vein we get to view the sailing dinghy races at close quarters from our executive box – *Voyager* doing service as one of the marker buoys – and watch in wonder as a Benneteau flying a Swiss ensign anchors very precisely between the two marker buoys that identify a marina's entrance, which causes havoc for boaters trying to get in and out.

Quiet anchorages are delightful and restful, but once in a while there's nothing to beat the diversions of a lively harbour. We are particularly engaged by the activity over at the Coastguard Station which is also a Recruit Training Centre. Trainees are on the march with small rucksacks on their backs. When they get where they are going they begin chanting.

Then a woman on a nearby sloop begins to pull in her anchor rope. It seems to take her a long time but she never looks in our direction. We have unwittingly offended independent-minded single-handed sailors in the past by offering assistance they do not want, so we do not interfere. Finally, with a mighty heave she raises her anchor but it is hooked onto a heavy duty chain attached to the harbour bottom.

We ask if she wants help and she says her husband has left and she's exhausted. We go over. I remain in the dinghy and tie a rope onto the chain while David goes on deck and uses the rope to lift the chain off the anchor. It takes only minutes. She is just offering her thanks when a power boat hurtles past sending her boat plunging, which hits our dinghy and nearly throws me overboard. She says she has reported them to the police, during her stay, for reckless driving but nothing was done.

It does seem extraordinary that under the nose of a Coast Guard training facility there is no attempt to control speed through the harbour beyond a sign saying *No Wake* on its dock. They are obviously too busy with the chanting. It goes on until after 9pm. We wonder if the cadets aren't rather weary by now.

After a long run down the harbour into town next day we discover that Cape May has no dinghy dock. This is just becoming a problem when a man with a yacht berthed in a marina calls over to say we can leave ours with him if we like.

The town is named after an early 17th century Dutchman, Cornelius Mey, who explored, charted and claimed the area as the province of New Netherland. It was later settled by New Englanders. By the mid 18th century Cape May was already welcoming holiday visitors from Philadelphia and is acknowledged today as the country's oldest seaside resort.

We take a long and very enjoyable walk to the post office, down Washington Street, part of the old town, with its large and elegant Victorian wooden houses. Their trees shade the sidewalk - huge magnolias, crab apple and Japanese maple – while their gardens are vibrant with hydrangeas, lilies and old-fashioned sunflowers.

There is a Model T 'Doctor's Coupe' on the lawn outside the museum, a former southern mansion, and further on an old fire station you can simply wander into, with a 1928 fire engine and early uniforms.

We shop at the store behind the fire station but have forgotten about the Liquor Laws. They vary around the country, and in this State you can buy only low strength beer in a supermarket. If you want wine, spirits or strong beer you have to go to a liquor store. Cape May's is some distance away but we have a special occasion coming up. David has planned somewhere for us to spend it and he wants a bottle of champagne to celebrate it.

The morning is becoming hot and he says it makes no sense for both of us to lug heavy rucksacks through it. So he leaves me in the shade with them and sets off on the long hike to the liquor store. While he is gone I am left to observe American shopping habits as a long procession of people pull up in their cars and drive away with only a beaker of take-out coffee.

Nowhere, in any of the umpteen countries through which we have travelled in recent years, have I ever seen anyone drive to a supermarket simply to buy a cup of coffee, or leave the engine running to keep the air-conditioning going while they shop; or even, in one case, leave the engine running, the air-conditioning going and the windows open so that the dog could stick its head out. The reason I have never seen it anywhere but here is the low cost of America's gasoline.

It is a hot and very bouncy journey back to *Voyager* thanks to the lack of speed control in the harbour. The chanting from the Coast Guard station goes on throughout the afternoon and evening without respite until after 9pm again. We can't help wondering where this fits in with rescuing those in peril on the sea.

41
Atlantic City to Manasquan Inlet

To continue on the inland waterway is no longer an option because there is a fixed bridge ahead which is too low for us to get under no matter what the state of the tide. So we leave Cape May harbour and go out to sea, for the first time this summer, on the seven-hour journey to Atlantic City. The day begins hazy but becomes hot and sunny later, with a light wind which allows us to motor sail.

The anchorage, when we reach it, has a surprisingly strong current running through it but also the advantage of good holding and the anchor bites quickly and securely. In fact, it is one of our fastest ever: the current sending *Voyager* hurtling backwards, and the anchor digging in so effectively that she is brought up with a mighty lurch. No testing necessary. Job done.

Atlantic City is famous for its boardwalk and its casinos. Thirty six of the latter, our book says. We end up anchored in the shadow of three of them: the Taj Mahal, Bally's and the Trump Plaza.

The boardwalk began as a means of keeping the sand out of the beach-front hotels and the railroad passenger cars. The original short, narrow stretch of wooden boards was laid down in 1870 and for some years was taken up at the end of each season and stored under cover for the winter. They can't do that now. The boardwalk is not only wider than it was but five-and-a-half miles long.

It is a Saturday night in late July – show time - so as well as the lights from the hotels and casinos twinkling on the water, there is a huge firework display ashore and an airship, brightly lit from within, flying along the coast.

At 6am, raising the anchor proves tricky because of the strong current, and initially we have a head wind of between five and ten knots. We pass a very long beach - eventually - because it is 18 miles long. It is the outer shore of a barrier island protecting Barnegat Bay, and a seemingly endless stretch of golden sand. A solitary pelican, our first sighting in a long while, seems to be its only resident.

Once past the Barnegat Inlet we alter course and are able to put out a sail. Two black headed gulls float past on a small plank of wood. Our destination is Manasquan Inlet and we arrive around mid-afternoon.

Once inside the inlet we turn hard to port down a narrow channel past the Coast Guard station and moored shrimp boats to the 300-ft long dock in front of the Shrimp Box Restaurant.

We have spent our nights in many places since we set off up the ICW in May – salt marsh, mudflat, river, creek, lake, lagoon, a power station's cooling pond, a military camp and the bottom of people's gardens – but this is our first venture into the centre of a holiday resort and commercial fishery. Holidaymakers and shrimp boat men alike turn to observe *Voyager*'s unfamiliar lines make their way to a vacant berth.

Nosing in among fishing trawlers and various commercial pleasure craft - a faux stern-wheeler and some charter fishing boats - we take the only space left, behind a yacht from Texas. There is no power or water available, but *Skipper Bob* says this is a free dock if you spend $20 or more in the restaurant.

'Not anymore,' says the manager. 'Insurance.'

So we hand over a $20 berthing fee and re-think our plans for dinner. We wander off to the sea front and stroll along the boardwalk on Point Pleasant Beach. One section of it looks down onto some very desirable beach homes built directly onto the sand.

America, on the whole, has not yet embraced the notion of climate change and rising sea levels, but looking at these houses on the leeward side of the boardwalk, built well below the level of the beach, you can't help wondering about their vulnerability. Especially given the amount of weather anomalies we have encountered these last two years. In more than a dozen countries people have said, 'This is not usual at this time of year.' Or, 'I can't ever remember anything like this before.'

The most dramatic for us was last November. We were in the Canary Islands, waiting to cross the Atlantic to the Caribbean, when two weeks after the time-honoured end of the North Atlantic hurricane season a monster called Lenny turned up and trashed large areas of the Caribbean. Not merely was it out of season but unusually, and for maximum damage, it travelled from west to east, thereby hitting the towns and resorts built on what is normally the sheltered side of the islands.

After the residential part of Point Pleasant Beach come the fun palaces. American holiday resorts and European ones are not unalike. This one has fast food stalls, fairground attractions, side shows, fortune tellers' booths, tossing plastic frogs onto plastic lily pads for prizes, and the dodgems – only here the little cars are racing M&Ms, a favourite US candy better known to Britons as Smarties.

On the way back to *Voyager* we buy some bluefish off one of the boats and dine in the cockpit, looking about us. This is a lovely billet. And as a soft blue evening descends we watch the holiday boats set out. Two fishing boats carry young men, striking macho poses, off to prove their mettle with rod and line.

Meanwhile the paddle steamer, whose wheel doesn't quite touch the water, embarks on a Friday night, ballroom-of-dreams scenario, with single men leaning moodily against the bows and women huddled at the stern. But, in the general manner of these things, a drink or two and the sparkle of lights on the water in the gathering darkness promises a more sociable return.

Next morning it is a bit of a squeeze getting off the pontoon as another yacht has rafted up to the Texan boat in front of us overnight. But at least it gives us an opportunity to put a manoeuvre called 'the spring' into practice and using a forward engine and a rope round a pontoon cleat we spring ourselves out of the tight space.

The sun rises deep red in a hazy, partly cloudy sky. We breakfast at sea. Being Saturday, its surface is awash with men in small fishing boats. I have often thought how similar in function the coastal-dweller's dinghy is - in terms of escaping the domestic weekend grind - to the inland-dweller's garden shed.

42
New Jersey Hospitality

Forty miles on we enter New Jersey's huge Sandy Hook Bay and David radios up a marina to see if its fuel dock is open. It is, and he is careful to stress that *Voyager* is 40 feet long and 16 feet wide in case this is a marina for small boats and difficult to get in and out of.

No comment is made about our size, but it turns out to be a cramped little fuel dock in a corner up a dead end with nowhere to turn round to get out again. We have little choice, however, being down to our last eggcupful of diesel. David does well to squeeze us in among the moored boats but things are just beginning to get a little tricky when two silver-haired men materialize, take our lines, guide us in and tie us up. Then they haul over the hoses for diesel and water and hand them to us. We are very grateful but wonder at this rather high ratio of staff for a small marina.

They turn out to be a retired international banker and a former chief of police, both of whom keep boats here. The ex-banker offers to drive one of us to the supermarket while our tanks fill, which is lovely as the convenience store in Cape May was a bit limited and the town of Leonardo – at three or four miles away – would have been too long a walk for a hot day.

If I'd had any doubts that the man driving me into town in his station wagon really was a retired international banker they evaporate after I mention the high price of Britain's fuel compared to America, and in five seconds flat he has mentally converted pence-per-litre into cents-per-US-gallon. That would have taken me several days with a calculator and even then there'd have been no guarantee.

He asks me about what we are doing and I tell him, and how one of the contributors to my decision was the American polar explorer, Richard Evelyn Byrd. Someone had sent me a birthday card containing a quote from him just at the time when I, an Olympic-standard hoarder, had been faced with the prospect of disposing of most of my worldly goods. Byrd had written: *Half the confusion in the world comes from not knowing how little we need. I live more simply now and am happier.*

'An *American* said that?' the former international banker asks wryly. And, I have to admit, I can't help wondering what Richard Byrd would have made of shopping malls.

With regard to shopping, I have a question of my own: 'Why are you doing this?' He wanted us to have a warm feeling about Leonardo, he says, and winces as we pass a suspected drug dealer having his car searched by members of the local police department.

Back at the marina, with our tanks filled, and our provisions loaded on board, the two men untie us and David eases *Voyager* away from the cramped little dock. As we sidle out backwards the former police chief calls, 'Stop in for a beer on your way back south.'

A little later, as we approach our chosen anchorage, Horseshoe Cove, a trawler yacht skipper calls us up on the VHF to warn us that we are approaching a sand bar, just as we go aground on it. So, after dropping the anchor to stop us drifting we have to wait for the tide to come in.

'I did wonder briefly,' I say to David, 'if they really were an international banker and a police chief.'

He gives me one of those looks he uses when he expects something bizarre or obscure to follow.

'I mean, you aren't supposed to just swan off with strange men, are you? They could have been people traffickers.'

He shakes his head. 'Too old.'

What's their age got to do with it?

'Not theirs. Yours.'

Observing a flight of birds passing overhead I say darkly, 'Dinner in the duck then?' and head for the galley.

It really had been a super supermarket and gorged on hot barbecued chicken and cold beer, glorious mahogany-red cherries, cheese buns and big mugs of tea, we both fall asleep. When we wake the water has risen enough to move off the shoal to a better depth and re-anchor.

Sandy Hook is part of the Gateway National Recreation Area, a vast network of parkland, nature trails, wildlife refuges and beaches. With a seawall protecting it from the Atlantic, it is a popular place for boaters, walkers and swimmers.

It also claims to have one of the largest 'clothing optional' beaches on the east coast, which makes it the only nude beach we have so far encountered since nudity is not something much associated with American leisure activities. Unlike parts of Europe where sometimes the sights are so appalling you just *will* some people to put some clothing on.

NEW YORK STATE

43
New York Harbour

Today is July 31 and two years to the day since we embarked on our new life afloat. I can see us now, staggering down a long marina pontoon in the south of England carrying everything short of the kitchen sink to load onto *Voyager*. And we hadn't been exactly what you could call afloat at the time either. It was a drying berth during a period of very low tides and it took over a week for her hulls to stagger up from the mud before we could set sail for France.

Our destination now is New York Harbour. But as we prepare to leave Sandy Hook Bay, and enter the harbour's lower reaches, we can see nothing ahead but a bank of fog with the top of a freighter's superstructure sticking out of it. It looks eerie out there, and dangerous, so we turn back and re-anchor. A fog horn drones mournfully all morning. After lunch, however, the sun comes out for a bit and with visibility improved we set off again.

The big open expanse of Lower New York Bay is dotted with men on fishing trips, either in large groups standing shoulder to shoulder on big motor cruisers, or individuals in small day boats, many of them drifting happily in the various navigation lanes. We follow the Chapel Hill Channel, dodging freighters and other commercial vessels.

We pass Coney Island on our right-hand side, famous for its seaside resort and amusement parks, although it is not technically an island. Originally an outer barrier island, it was joined to the mainland by landfill.

Lower Bay begins to narrow. To stay clear of the traffic – some very large, very fast ships - we begin to hug the right-hand shore as we go under the aptly named Narrows Bridge, connecting Brooklyn with Staten Island. It is a double-decker bridge and there is the most tremendous roar from the road traffic as you pass under it.

Our progress is rather slow. It is only five months since we scraped and anti-fouled *Voyager*'s hulls but already she is beginning to foul up and this is reducing our speed considerably. Part of the reason is that manufacturers of anti-fouling paint have reduced the copper content. This is good for the environment but it makes the paint less effective. It is also an eroding paint, and we have done a lot of mileage since we last anti-fouled her in Antigua. We need to think about another haul-out.

We are now in the Upper Bay of New York Harbour. There is sporadic rain, the wind has risen to 21 knots and it is surprisingly cold. Visibility is also very poor and this huge harbour is filled with very large vessels, some anchored and some moving very slowly. It can be hard to judge which, and the situation is further confused when tugs suddenly burst into life and begin shunting massive barges around.

David listens in to Channel 13, the one the harbour pilots use, which helps a little to work out what is about to move where. There is also a regular buffeting from the passenger ferries and tourist boats rushing through the harbour between Manhattan, Staten Island, Sandy Hook and the Statue of Liberty.

We finally spot the Statue of Liberty through the mist, and then gradually Manhattan Island beyond it. The channel to our anchorage requires a sharp left in front of the statue and just as we approach the turn the *Queen Elizabeth II* sails past on her way out to sea.

It is rather nice. Two British vessels together like that, flying the Red Ensign. The *QEII*: 963 feet long, 105 feet wide, around 70,000 tons and 1,000 officers and crew plus passengers. *Voyager*: 40 feet long, 16 feet wide and 10 tons. I doubt anyone even notices us. I wave anyway.

We settle into the little anchorage under the statue for the night. The wind falls away and everywhere is still. The only sound is the patter of rain.

Today is our 36th wedding anniversary and we had already decided what we wanted to do with it before we arrived here. We have just spent some hot, busy days in Annapolis and a hot and hectic week in Washington before that. And, the cold and wet of yesterday notwithstanding, we know that the Big Apple is famous for its steaming August temperatures.

What we both *really* fancy now is a self-indulgent day. And we couldn't have a better spot for it: a New York Harbour frontage with all its comings and goings, the trees of Liberty State Park at their summer best and the massive Statue of Liberty towering above them. The statue stands on its own small island and it depends on the state of the tide how much of her is visible from our anchorage. At high tide we can see her from the waist up; at low tide only her extended right arm and the torch.

After yesterday's cold, wet and blustery conditions, by mid-morning it is delightful out in the cockpit, hot enough for swimsuits and very, very still. A heron flies overhead and arctic terns dive for food around us. Apart from a couple of anglers on the Jersey Shore, and someone walking a dog through the park, we are quite alone. And to dine, thanks to the unexpected thoughtfulness of two Sandy Hook retirees and the bounty of Leonardo's supermarket, we have one of our favourite meals to look forward to – filet steak with mushrooms - plus some delicious dessert. And a bottle of champagne. Oh, the joys of sailing! How else could you stay for free in New York, with prime views and the Statue of Liberty thrown in?

We leave the anchorage just after 6am, sidling down the narrow channel beside Liberty State Park which is as shallow as five feet in places. We need to leave at this time in the morning to reach Hell Gate, approximately ten miles away, at the right state of the tide. There is a strong current there, which needs to be taken within two hours of slack water.

We bear left at the Statue of Liberty, with a red sun rising behind it, and cross the Upper Bay, dodging the Staten Island ferries in the mist. Conditions are so changeable. Two days ago we arrived in a cold, wet and windswept harbour; spent yesterday in windless warmth and sunshine; while today is cool and visibility poor.

To our left is Ellis Island. The famous immigrant inspection station - with its impressive high walls and four domed towers - is now a museum. It was here, from 1892 until 1954, that immigrants disembarked from passenger ships to be assessed for entry into America. Although the process was not quite as altruistic as suggested by Emma Lazarus whose 1883 poem includes the famous line, 'Give me your tired, your poor, your huddled masses.'

Only those fit for work and able to support themselves were accepted. Those deemed likely to become a drain on the public purse were rejected, including some of the unskilled, the old and the sick who were either sent back to their country of origin or held in the island's hospital, often for long periods. Over 3,000 would-be immigrants died there and not for nothing was Ellis Island also known as Heartbreak Island.

But it had happier associations for the millions beginning a new life or those greeting friends and family members come to join them. It is estimated that today over 100 million Americans, or a third of the population, can trace their ancestry to those arriving at Ellis Island before dispersing across the country.

To our right is Governors Island, with its circular fortification called Castle Williams and a stately-looking residence. Manhattan looms ahead.

First The Battery, the southern tip of the island, named for the artillery batteries that once protected the early settlement and now 25 acres of parkland.

It is a strange feeling. The harbour, the buildings and the names are all so well known from books, films and songs. And yet to be here, in a relatively small boat under your own steam, in this huge, *huge* harbour is inexplicably exciting. I stand on the foredeck and feel like a child on a first memorable outing.

We are now on the East River, with Manhattan's towering buildings on the left and Brooklyn on the right. We move over to the Brooklyn shore to avoid Manhattan's busy Pier 11 ferry terminal, just south of Wall Street, with its constantly arriving and departing ferries and excursion boats. From out here on the water you are also very aware of the 'canyons' they talk about between Manhattan's buildings. Meantime, the sea mist thickens.

Our route takes us under three impressive suspension bridges, all quite close together: the Brooklyn, the Manhattan and the Williamsburg.

The Brooklyn Bridge, completed in 1883, was one of the great engineering feats of its time because it is a very long suspension bridge built when suspension bridges had a history of spectacular failure. Untypically, its two supports were sunk into the river bed instead of the shore, requiring the development of new building techniques to construct them.

After the third bridge, the East River forks around either side of Roosevelt Island. We take the west channel, with Manhattan to our left, by which time visibility has been reduced to 200 yards.

It comes as a surprise to discover that along with the well-known ones - Manhattan, Coney, Ellis and Staten - there are 33 islands in the waters surrounding New York although few seem to have happy associations.

Roosevelt Island was formerly called Welfare Island because prisoners and the mentally ill were kept there and it once housed a penitentiary, a lunatic asylum, a workhouse, a smallpox hospital and a charity hospital. As we pass it, a ruined building looms up out of the mist and makes you feel, even after all this time, how unutterably defeating incarceration in this place must have been.

The Queensboro Bridge, also known as the 59th Street Bridge - made famous by Simon and Garfunkel's *59th Street Bridge Song* – passes over Roosevelt Island between Manhattan and Long Island City in Queens. Running parallel with this bridge's north side is a cable car, or what

Americans call a tram way, operating between Roosevelt Island and Manhattan. It is not on our chart because it is higher than the bridge and therefore no threat to shipping. But as we clear the bridge and look up we are quite startled to see a large gondola, or tram, capable of carrying 110 passengers, gliding overhead.

The East River has been placid until now, but as we leave the north end of Roosevelt Island the water starts to become agitated. We have reached the beginning of an infamous one-mile stretch.

Other tidal races we have sailed through have names taken from their environment: for example, the Alderney Race in the Channel Islands, France's Raz de Seine, and Ramsey Sound in Wales. With typical chutzpah New Yorkers invoke the nether regions and call theirs Hell Gate.

Ideally we should have left our Liberty State Park anchorage at the bottom of the tide, which would have enabled us to reach this stretch of waterway at the optimum time. Unfortunately, that would have meant leaving the anchorage in darkness, with only unlit buoys to mark the narrow channel through shallow water.

By waiting for first light we are an hour later entering this tidal strait than we would have liked. There are dramatic swirls and eddies already pulling us this way and that and requiring constant attention to the steering. Had we been able to start at the ideal time we should have come through here at a more controlled pace. As it is, the current is pushing us along at five knots faster than we could wish. But in these conditions it is not simply a matter of reducing engine speed because, if you do, you lose control of the boat and are tossed about at the whim of the currents. At its height the water in Hell Gate is fast and violent enough to spin smaller boats around in a circle.

Although a relatively short stretch of water, it was once littered with so many rocks that hundreds of vessels had sunk in it by the mid 19th century. In 1851 the US Army Corps of Engineers started a task which took decades to complete, blasting rocks and sunken ships out of the way. Its largest explosion took place in 1885 when they used 300,000lbs of explosives to destroy Flood Rock and created in the process a geyser of water 250 feet high.

As you pass through, facing you is Wards Island with the Harlem River to the left and the East River forking to the right. We stay on the East River, in very little traffic fortunately given that visibility is so poor. As a matter of fact, it is not a stretch of water I would relish in crowded conditions in any weather – especially if they were large commercial vessels.

We pass under two more bridges and then to the north of three islands, the largest of which is Rikers – the mere mention of the name a spur to a suspect's co-operation in many a New York Police drama. Its ten jails house prisoners serving sentences of one year or less, as well as local people awaiting trial in the Bronx courts who cannot make bail.

Just beyond Rikers Island is a *very* long jetty sticking out from the end of La Guardia airport to keep high-masted vessels away from its flight path. We can hear planes taking off and landing until finally we are close enough to see them.

By the time we enter Long Island Sound we have moved beyond thick mist and are now into fog. So instead of attempting to go any further today we head for City Island, anchoring at 9.30am on its south-west side to the sound of heavy gunfire which continues all day and well into the evening. The Long Island duck hunting season runs from November to March so heaven knows what is taking such a hit in August. But America does love its guns.

44
City Island, Long Island Sound

Long Island Sound is a 120-mile estuary with Long Island, New York State, forming the south shore and Connecticut the north.

This huge, relatively protected area provides sailors from both States with easy access to ocean sailing. It has strong currents, however, so some planning is needed, unlike the ICW – and even Chesapeake - where you can more or less point at a bit of chart and say, 'We'll go there tomorrow afternoon.'

Long Island itself stretches 118 miles from New York Harbour to a point level with the eastern border of Connecticut. While its western end contains the boroughs of Brooklyn and Queens, its north-eastern end is famed as a popular summer resort and the haunt of the very rich. In particular The Hamptons, a group of villages and hamlets, boast some of the most expensive homes in the US.

Our own location is pretty peaceful until around half past four when I notice a white buoy with orange wording saying 'Submerged Cable' close to our starboard hull. We don't understand how we could have failed to see it when we anchored. However, despite nothing being shown on our chart we feel we must move because it is illegal to drop an anchor onto a submerged electricity cable.

We take a look around us and decide the best place for us to go, but when we peer over the rail to check the buoy's exact location to avoid snagging it with our propeller, we can't see it anymore. We spend some time in the dinghy squinting under Voyager in case it is already tangled around our prop, before finally spotting it sitting alongside another yacht some distance away. It is a floater.

It is fortunate that we don't need to move because on climbing back aboard a squall hits us. Neither of us had seen it coming because we had both been crouched in the dinghy staring under our boat. It is so violent that the little revolving plastic cups at the top of our mast – which register wind speed on our instrument panel – become jammed from spinning too fast.

However, every squall has a silver lining because, when it has passed over, our television reception is superb. Nobody makes sit-coms like America – Cheers, Friends, Frazier, Golden Girls – and as we laugh we don't know that we are watching the end of its Golden Age.

We had intended leaving next morning but the weather forecast is for more rain. Visibility is already quite poor and it promises to be a dreary, uncomfortable journey so it seems sensible to stay where we are. But before the rain arrives we decide to go ashore and have a look around.

Despite its Bronx address, City Island has been likened to a small New England fishing village with nowhere on it far from the water. It has also been described as a place where fishing is an excuse to drift along in a boat in the sun and drink beer.

Had we set off in a clockwise direction around the island we should have encountered the New England fishing village. Unfortunately, we go anticlockwise. A man at a marina says people are not allowed to leave their dinghies there and that it is five blocks to anywhere anyway and best if we keep going. So we do. The day is becoming heavy and humid and not a good one for walking long distances, leaving us happy to dawdle along the shoreline instead. Every wooden pile along the way seems to have a cormorant on it: wings outstretched to dry its flight feathers, comical yellow beak gaping skywards.

After a while we estimate that somewhere beyond this bit of waterfront there must be some sort of town centre by now. And anyway, it is the only place we have seen where a landfall is possible. So we aim the dinghy towards a rundown collection of piles and pontoons that is home to an aging live-aboard yacht and some houseboats with flaking shingles bearing names like *The Good Life* and *Carpe Diem*. There are also a number of *Beware the Dog* notices so we hesitate before disembarking.

With no sign of a guard dog, however, or people either, we clamber out of the dinghy clutching four days' worth of domestic refuse and make our way up a listing pontoon toward the road, hoping nobody takes off with our dinghy while we're away or we shall really be in trouble.

After decorously disposing of our gash bags we have a look around. It seems more urban suburb than picturesque fishing village but having taken a stroll around we enter City Island Supermarket and find it a friendly place. New York, it has often been said, is a melting pot and no less so than in here. Eastern Europe restocks the meat counter, China operates the till, Latin America packs the bags, Italia pushes a mop.

Never miss an opportunity. This is a given of the cruising lifestyle whenever a well-stocked supermarket hoves into view. There are always a few staples you can do with, and when you carry your entire needs on your back it helps if you pace yourself.

Actually, despite the amount we do carry on our backs, it never fails to surprise us how often we need to shop. In fact, we have even wondered if somebody else might be availing themselves of our fridge and food cupboards; and whether they are the same people who leave all the washing-up that always seems to be piling up in the galley sink.

On the news later, the weatherman looks out over a deserted Yankee Stadium and says, 'It's not actually raining yet, but look at that *sky*! Dorothy and Toto just went past.'

We go and stare out through our bow windows at what looks like an orange tornado rising up behind Throgs Neck. It slowly glides towards us then hovers overhead, pancake-flat with ragged edges, a swirling battleship grey gradually deepening to blue-black. Lightning begins to snake down from it. And then rain. This has not been the sort of summer we were expecting.

For three hours after leaving City Island next day we can still see the Manhattan skyline directly behind us, until the buildings finally melt into the haze. On the way we pass a large derelict building and a huge industrial chimney on the ironically-named Heart Island. In its time this island has housed prisons, a Civil War internment camp, a hospital, a workhouse, a reformatory and a Nike missile base. Its current use is as a potter's field, from the biblical term for a common grave, and used now as a cemetery for unknown or indigent people.

There are lots of cormorants. The water is very dirty. The sky is overcast for a long time, until late afternoon when the cloud thins and the sun turns the day quite hot.

Looking at the chart, and given how much of our visa allocation has already expired, we estimate that we have only about a month left before we must begin heading south again. Within this time we need to allow for a haul-out to get *Voyager*'s hull scraped and antifouled. And we have also been looking forward to cruising Maine. So regrettably we cannot afford to linger among the attractions of Long Island Sound.

One of them is Port Jefferson on its North Shore, a large and very sheltered bay thanks to an encircling headland and a narrow entrance. We anchor early evening, rather tired, so make a quick meal of ravioli and pesto sauce and end up dining under one of the most spectacular sunsets we have ever seen. The sun is huge and a deep, vibrating red. It points a wide finger of shimmering light across the water that changes imperceptibly from crimson to gold by the time it reaches our starboard quarter.

After the sun sinks there is a strange green light on the water for a while until crimson clouds dapple the green with red. Then gradually the sky, the water and everything on it, including us, becomes rose madder. It is hypnotic. You couldn't leave it and go and do something useful below, even if you wanted to. You just have to sit there, *bathed* in it.

We wake before dawn. The harbour is wonderfully still and after yesterday's slow passage David thinks conditions would be ideal to go over the side and remove some of the encrustation, at least from the propellers. I look down at the unspeakable material floating by and plead against it. He consults the chart which shows a sewage outlet at the far end of the harbour. He decides to wait for cleaner water.

On the VHF the Coast Guard can be heard trying to persuade leisure boats to slow down as they supervise a 15-mile swimming relay race across Long Island Sound. It is the annual race from Port Jefferson on the New York side, to Bridgeport on the Connecticut side, and takes place on whichever weekend in late July or early August has the most appropriate tides.

Just beyond the harbour entrance around forty small support craft are gathered, many with balloons flying, and just discernible among them is the occasional flash of a human arm doing the crawl. The Coast Guard continues to plead for passing boats to restrict their speed and be aware of swimmers but to little avail.

CONNECTICUT

45
Milford, Noank and Mystic

Across Long Island Sound, on the Connecticut shore, is Milford. Its harbour is dominated by small fishing boats and oystermen and lots of leisure boats either on buoys or in marinas. It is very crowded, as might be expected on an August weekend, so we head for its outer bay known as The Gulf. It has two long, curving beaches and some very attractive houses. We are the only boat around.

The western side of this bay has a causeway, visible only at low tide, which leads to Charles Island. We anchor in the shelter of this small, wooded island and David says that tomorrow morning he will go over the side and scrape off some crustaceans.

A news report on Fox late evening says a number of Connecticut beaches, including Milford, are closed to bathers because of the bacteria levels (David decides not to go over the side tomorrow after all); there have been a number of cases of E-coli, one of them fatal; and an incidence of West Nile Virus. A tornado is also on its way from Idaho, although the winds should have abated by the time it reaches Connecticut and will simply mean days of rain. We wonder if Connecticut is the place to be at present.

In the event the new day dawns dry and bright and this is a pretty spot. At low tide a few people walk along the causeway to Charles Island. One couple, pushing a child's buggy, have to stop every now and then and wait for the tide to fall a bit more so that they can continue. Anglers cast their lines from it and a couple of women wade in to collect shellfish. Although I can't help feeling that if it's unsafe to swim in this stuff perhaps you shouldn't be eating what's been living in it either.

It is a long, leisurely sail to Noank next day, not least because of the impedimenta on *Voyager*'s hull. Even the bathroom sink empties slowly since something took up residence in its outlet pipe.

You enter Noank through a channel between rocks and islands, one group of which has small dwellings on it. The route to the anchorage goes close to the village. Built on a tradition of fishing, lobstering and boat-building it has lots of jetties and pilings, lobster restaurants and crab shacks and rising up behind the houses a white church steeple.

The anchorage is shallow and densely buoyed but we find a spot to drop our anchor. A train runs close to the shore, with half a dozen carriages looking like aluminium cigar tubes. Its engine makes a sound like a slide trombone.

What we are looking for is facilities suitable for lifting *Voyager* out so that we can scrape and antifoul her hulls. The Noank boatyards can't oblige so the plan is to telephone those around Mystic, another small town further up the river. Unfortunately, when we try, the mobile's screen shows 'Extended Area', meaning we can only get the numbers we want by paying to do so by credit card because AT&T don't have an agreement with the local cell phone company.

Unfortunately, as we have already discovered, US telephone companies won't accept British credit cards. So, off we go on what turns out to be a very long but picturesque dinghy ride up the Mystic River.

The travel lift at the first yard we try is two inches narrower than *Voyager*. At the next one the receptionist quotes a horrendous amount to lift our boat and then refers us to someone out in the yard for the rest of the charges (power washing, hard standing fees, etc) but he isn't around so we'll have to come back later. By this time we've lost interest anyway. At these prices it would be cheaper to buy a new boat.

With nowhere else to try we go and have a look around Mystic, with its tiny town hall and the restaurant which gave its name to the Julia Roberts movie *Mystic Pizza*. As well as a historic colonial village it is also home to a 17-acre maritime museum with some wonderfully restored buildings and vessels.

By now it has become hot and humid but the boat ride home provides a refreshing breeze and a couple of boat names to treasure. Retirees, an American yachtsman told us, often name their boats after some aspect of their earlier life. For example, *Postage Due* is a favourite with former members of the postal service.

So, along with general collectables, we are always on the look-out for names with professional associations, and when we spotted a square, two-storey houseboat recently called *This Side Up,* we assumed an owner with a parcel delivery connection.

Among today's offerings, *Route Canal* suggests an orthodontist with a touch of whimsy, while *Sloop du Jour* has echoes of the restaurant trade.

RHODE ISLAND

46
Block Island

We leave Noank in a gentle morning expecting a quiet sail to Block Island and are immediately surrounded by members of a yacht club bent on racing - to Block Island. Among them are a couple of large, traditional motor yachts carrying committee members acting as race organisers and judges, in naval-type uniforms and peaked caps and saluting each other.

Since racing yachts are penalized if they cross the start line before the signal, these wheel about jockeying for position and causing some irritation among the local shrimp boats. One of them, forced off course amid billowing sails, yells over Channel 16, 'Why don't ya take up the *whole* channel?'

'That's rich from a fisherman!' comes the reply.

Inevitably this many yachts are going to put pressure on Block Island's anchorage. There will be a stampede for available spaces and yachtsmen, psyched up from a race, can get pretty assertive. As it turns out, by the time the race gets going the wind has dropped away to almost nothing. We switch on an engine, which obviously they are not allowed to do, and make it to the anchorage well ahead of them. There is a decent spot close to shore, in water too shallow for their keels anyway.

Block Island is six and a half miles by three and a half, and shaped like a lamb chop. It takes its name from the 17th century Dutch explorer Adriaen Block and its anchorage, called Great Salt Pond, provides excellent shelter for boats. This is something for which we shall be grateful in coming days as the weather is about to turn nasty. And, being August, Great Salt Pond is due to get *very* crowded.

Although our bit of it is too shallow for the larger boats, we are soon deluged in smaller ones. Some hopeful newcomers accept that there really isn't room to insert even just *one* more in among those of us already in situ. Others squeeze in anyway, drop their anchor over somebody else's then wobble back almost onto the bow of the one behind.

The consensus is that we shall all be alright unless somebody drags more than three feet in the night. At least it is sociable; we are so close to each other that chatting with your neighbours is easy.

In between anchors dropping around him, David goes over the side to take a look at *Voyager*'s hulls and finds them a mass of razor-sharp barnacles. He decides to enquire about a diver when we go ashore. An irritable official sends us to a dive shop on the way into town. A mile and a half walk later an irritable woman there directs us back to virtually where we started. Continuing on into town we arouse the deepest suspicions of the woman at the library who watches us like a hawk all the time we are there. Two of our emails are long and full of news from home, so we pay to print them out and go and read them on the beach by the old harbour instead.

An elderly man there, seated beside an affable black Labrador, tells us about coming here for holidays as a boy and how much it has changed. There is a saying: *Never revisit the places of your youth.* This is especially true in high season.

Half way through the dinghy ride back to *Voyager* we remember about the diver, but decide not to bother. It can't be long now before we can get a haul-out. In the meantime our outboard engine sounds very sick, will not rev and regularly misses a beat. To keep us going forward I assist with a paddle. It makes it back - just about - and another job goes on the to-do list.

According to the weather forecast, Hurricane Alberto is approaching the south-east coast. Unfortunately even up here we will still get the fringe effects of it, with unpleasant conditions and a strong wind on the nose if we try to travel north; between 20 and 25 knots apparently, and rain. Connecticut, which we just left, has already had three inches of rainfall in an hour, presumably that downpour threatened by the Idaho tornado. The bad weather now approaching us is due to last three days. We decide to stay put.

The situation in the anchorage is fluid. Some people move – many for the short sail back to the mainland and home, given the weather - and others take their place. A late arrival is a bright yellow racing yacht called *Trapeze*. There are two men aboard who look like father and son. Both are big and cheery with loud voices and they manage to settle into a very small space without threatening anybody else's boat or anchor.

Their own boat is small, however, and being large themselves they spend most of the time in its tiny cockpit. It is very windy and not at all pleasant but they manage to cook a meal on their barbecue. Then they spread their mattresses along the side decks in the wind to dry, their clothing is draped in whatever space is left, and they sit smoking together in companionable silence.

There are very high winds for several days along with heavy showers of rain but at least Hurricane Alberto gives up on the US coast, turning north-east and back into the Atlantic. The two men on *Trapeze* set off under a howling sky saying they might not get beyond the harbour entrance.

I do some chores, change the bed linen and lay some dust. How you get quite so much dust living on water is an enduring mystery. David works on the outboard. Halfway through re-assembly he says he doesn't think he's going to have any bits left over. This is always a good sign. But by the time he thinks he might have it working again, and is ready to test it, the wind is roaring through the anchorage and the sky has turned black.

Trapeze returns, its crew saturated again. Americans have less annual holiday than Western Europeans. Apart from federal holidays most have only ten working days, whereas their European counterparts mostly get twenty, with some having thirty or more.

Watching the little boat's crew hanging out their clothing between downpours, David reflects on the difficulty of having only two weeks holiday when summer does this sort of thing to you. I am about to offer them a dry bed when they begin describing the height of the waves beyond the harbour with such gusto that it finally dawns on me that they are thoroughly enjoying all this.

The next deluge brings good TV reception in its wake, so we tune in. There are the usual game shows and shopping channels. And someone has cleverly combined these two national favourites into a programme called *Supermarket Sweep*. Its logo is a racing shopping cart.

There is also an increasing amount of political coverage; in particular the upcoming presidential campaign and the outgoing Clintons. Hilary is heavily criticised for the handling of her marriage, which seems a bit much in the circumstances.

On the news there are more reports of mosquito-borne West Nile Encephalitis and how incidents are increasing, and there is a tropical storm called Beryl in the Gulf of Mexico which is currently heading for Texas. The limitations of a 5-inch black-and-white TV screen are at their most apparent when a meteorologist points to a weather map the size of a postage-stamp and says, 'The green areas you can see here are rain.'

American television has longer advertising breaks than Britain. Among its regular advertisers are pharmaceutical companies and something they are scrupulous about is advising on a drug's side-effects. In Britain, with its National Health Service, the objective is to keep costs down by using generic drugs wherever possible. Any marketing campaigns by pharmaceutical companies for specific drugs are therefore aimed at the medical profession and a new digital clock/calendar on a GP's reception counter - bearing the brand name of the latest anti-depressant - is a sure sign that a drug company rep has recently passed through.

In America, patients can ask their doctor to prescribe whatever type or brand they want as long as they, or their insurance company, are prepared to pay for it. Accordingly there are massive advertising campaigns aimed at the public. But, whatever the ailment or the offered solution is, the drug companies include any known side effects, however rare. This can have unintentionally hilarious results when the drug is for something you didn't even know was a medical condition in the first place, such as shyness.

Our favourite has a soft, optimistic voice murmuring over images of forlorn individuals: 'If social anxiety is destroying *your* confidence and making *your* life miserable, ask your doctor about X'.

Then, as these unhappy people, loitering on the periphery of life, suddenly blossom into fulfilling relationships thanks to X, the voice continues in the same soft, upbeat murmur: 'Side effects may include impotence, night sweats, indigestion, bladder infections, memory loss, balance-impairment, temporary deafness and vomiting.'

None of which sounds at all conducive to building an individual's confidence, a social life, or the intimate personal relationship that prompted the use of this medication in the first place.

The list of possible side effects for drugs may not only be very long but can culminate in horrendous possibilities such as permanent blindness, suicidal tendencies and physical complications leading to death. However, the reading of it is speeded up to such a degree that the mind can barely register these potential outcomes. The worst, rare-but-possible ones are left to the very end, by which time they are little more than a blur. On the other hand, as a National Health Service patient, I don't remember ever being told about side effects at all.

The days are windy and cold with constant rain. Our upholstery feels damp and we are both wearing several layers of clothing. On the plus side

Beryl has weakened and is dissipating, unable to sustain winds above 35 knots and reduced to a minor gale. Alberto, a mere shadow of his former self since diverting into the Atlantic, has been downgraded to a tropical storm.

We get up one morning to a blue sky with a few scattered white clouds and think about making a run for it. But by the time we have waited for the tide to turn the sky is charcoal grey, there is thunder about and the wind is 20 knots on the nose and rising. So we decide not to bother. Fortunately our food cupboards are well stocked.

Interestingly, America does not currently put a sell-by date on food, not even meat and dairy produce which seems strange to us, although they do on beer which seems even stranger. American beer comes with a six-month shelf-life and its cans carry the words, 'Born on:' followed by the date on which it was brewed.

One evening a blue-hulled sloop arrives among us and comes to a halt. A young man walks forward, picks up a bundle of rope with an anchor on the top, and drops the lot over the bow.

The final arrival of the night is a ketch whose skipper squeezes into an untenable space by putting out three anchors to keep himself off the blue-hulled sloop, us and some rusting rails running from the shore into the water. Then he goes ashore in his dinghy.

We are getting ready for bed when we notice that the ketch is wearing the small sloop on its stern. The man on the boat in front of us dutifully gets into his dinghy and rows over to the two boats currently locked together. He climbs aboard the unoccupied ketch but forgets to tie up his dinghy first and it floats away. We prepare to go and rescue it. I put my clothes back on and David is lowering our dinghy when someone zooms past in his inflatable and saves us the trouble.

Including the two people already on the sloop there are now four people sorting out the problem and that seems enough, so I take off my clothes and prepare for bed again. The wind shifts and there is quite a bit of shouting from the two boats and I put my clothes back on. By the look of it, the ketch has dislodged the anchor of the sloop.

We are about to get into the dinghy when another inflatable zooms past and we recognize the owner of the ketch, back from his evening ashore. As I stand wondering if it is safe to take my clothes off again, the island's launch passes our stern and decants several more men onto the two boats. I return to bed but cannot sleep.

Around midnight I watch the ketch's skipper shunting, shifting and juggling his three anchors, until finally he gives up and motors away. I still can't go to sleep. An hour later I look out of the window just inches from my feet and think how uncommonly close to land we are. As my brain gets into gear and I begin to rise from our bunk, so *Voyager*'s starboard hull bumps against the shore. We quickly realize that returning to our old spot is not an option. A number of other boats have also dragged – into our space - and there is no longer room for us to reset our anchor safely.

We end up in much deeper water not far from the wandering ketch. The holding is poor here and it starts to wander again, along with several other boats, so I keep watch until 4am when it becomes apparent that we have begun to drag as well, albeit very slowly. However, by the time I've woken David and told him there is no need to hurry, we are going fast.

With the wind at twenty knots we trawl round and round trying not only to find suitable space and depth but also somewhere the anchor will bite. Finally we find an ideal place with nobody in it and after keeping watch for a while, the wind falls away and we finally go to bed. We are roused by the Coast Guard telling us we are anchored in a forbidden area and must move. Although sluggish and tired, it is a timely awakening for us to catch the tide out.

We have been most grateful for the shelter Block Island has provided during a period of unseasonably bad weather, but we are not sorry to be going. It is not the island's fault. It is simply a very popular destination for the many boat owners of Rhode Island, Connecticut and Massachusetts and a peak holiday period to boot. It is also our first real encounter with overcrowding in a long time and we have become spoiled. We put up the genoa and take turns to get a little sleep.

MASSACHUSETTS

47
Buzzards Bay

The plan is to spend the night at Cuttyhunk Island, just inside Buzzards Bay. The route to get there, through Rhode Island Sound, is a cluttered one according to the chart. It shows traffic separation zones for commercial shipping (which we can only traverse at right angles), while dotted all around are warnings of unexploded depth charges. Then there's a dumping ground (for what it doesn't say), a torpedo range and a restricted area (for what reason it is unclear but we decide we had better avoid it anyway).

With all these hazards we make a zigzag passage but, as we finally approach the entrance to Buzzards Bay, way off to our right we can see Martha's Vineyard and beyond it Nantucket Island.

Sailing up the narrow channel into Cuttyhunk Harbour we encounter a phenomenon to which most of us will have succumbed at some time in our lives. That is: having planned something – in this case a seaside holiday – you embark on all the traditional things associated with it, even though the weather and the chosen environment conspire against the desired outcome.

Accordingly there are two people shivering in deckchairs on a narrow strip of sand and a girl whose determination to swim is frustrated by constantly passing boats. We are necessarily one of them, but the harbour is so crowded that after circling it a couple of times without finding anywhere to drop our anchor we go back outside – past the thwarted young swimmer again - and anchor in the bay. It is a quiet night out there, bathed in moonlight.

Every now and then nature takes you by surprise. Heading north up Buzzards Bay next morning the water is flat and shiny, until suddenly I realize I can see an approaching breeze even though I can't feel it yet.

Where the breeze has already reached, the surface of the water resembles the cross-hatching on a silver engraving plate. I watch the edge of it approaching our bow, a straight line across the water: on the far side of the line a pattern; on ours it is clear as glass.

I read once that there is no such thing as a straight line in nature. Well, there is. When this one reaches our bows it breaks briefly, reconnects behind our stern and continues. And for a while we motor on flat, cross-hatched water, the pattern reflecting the silvery sunlight, until the wind increases and breaks it into wavelets.

A name that leaps off the chart today is Scraggy Neck, especially as this particular promontory, or neck, is circular and wooded and not scraggy at all. Once past it, the traffic starts to get busier and the current stronger.

Our objective is the Cape Cod Canal and then up the Massachusetts coast. Unfortunately the very strong current in Buzzards Bay is against us and will prevent us catching a favourable tide through the canal at an appropriate time today. The sensible thing to do is make a detour into Onset Bay for the night and get to the Cape Cod Canal tomorrow when its tide will be running in the right direction for us.

At Onset, despite David not having any bits left over when he put the outboard engine back together, it refuses to start and we paddle ashore. It is a very attractive 19th century town without appearing to have been prettified. It also has a very decent supermarket for which we are grateful after so many days sheltering from bad weather at Block Island. Its owner volunteers his son to take us back to our dinghy in his car.

During the late afternoon, rows of terns sit on the pulpits of unoccupied boats. Even we get two, despite the fact that we are moving about on deck. One is a debutante, that is full-sized but with feathers that are not quite sleek yet and giving it a rumpled look.

Mature terns are beautiful birds, with their blisteringly white bodies and neat black caps, and balletic in flight. The mother of the debutante keeps trying to feed her highly vocal youngster but it flaps its wings and leaps about so much that the handing-over process becomes a shambles. Each little fish she brings it gets knocked from her beak and each time she goes off dutifully to catch another one.

At sunset there is a glorious orange sun that, as it sinks, paints the sky through all the shades from pale peach to deepest apricot. Then after dark, during one of his anchor checks, David calls me out into the cockpit. There is a huge semi-circle of flickering red lights. Candles have been lit on the shoreline all around the bay. Why, I cannot say. But it is quite magical, sitting in the darkness, like being in a charmed place.

48
Cape Cod

Seven miles long, the Cape Cod Canal has been cut through a neck of land that joins Cape Cod to mainland Massachusetts. By connecting Buzzards Bay with Cape Cod Bay this canal enables sailors to avoid an outside passage which is fraught with shoals and violent storms. The idea was first mooted in 1623 by Myles Standish, a passenger on the *Mayflower* and an English military officer who played a leading role in the administration and defence of the Pilgrims' Plymouth Colony. It was finally built in 1914. It is very pleasant and neatly kept with a path along both banks and currently busy with joggers, cyclists, roller bladers and mothers with pushchairs.

Once out of the confines of the canal, Cape Cod Bay opens up into a large expanse of water which is almost circular thanks to the curving 25-mile peninsular which forms its Atlantic edge. We take a direct line across the middle of the bay to the far end of this peninsular and drop our anchor in Provincetown Harbour for the night.

Viewed from the harbour it looks a pretty town, with a very tall, Italian-style dragon tower dominating the skyline. It is too far to paddle ashore, so we decide to save the visit for our return journey - by which time we hope to have a functioning outboard engine - and set off for Salem, further up the coast, next morning.

Such is the shape and length of the spit which protects Provincetown Harbour from the sea that after an hour we are barely a mile closer to Salem and only the other side of the tall, slender tower we had anchored opposite the previous night. It is an uneventful passage, with very little wind and none of it from the right direction, and only enlivened by the sight of three terns rafting on a piece of wood.

Salem Harbour is an offshoot of the much bigger Salem Sound and well-protected. Because of this it is a popular area. On reaching the anchorage closest to the town we find it heavily buoyed and return to the mouth of the harbour near Naugus Head to anchor.

There are nine-foot tides here. There is also a dark history to this area which is so infamous that word association becomes automatic. In fact, few people hear the name 'Salem' without immediately thinking 'witch trials'.

49
Salem Witch Trials

Something that can seem inexplicable to an outside observer is a sudden eruption of conflict within a community that has apparently lived harmoniously for a long time. It happened here in Salem between January 1692 and May 1693. During that time 19 people were hanged, five died in prison and one was pressed to death. Altogether, as many as two hundred were accused of witchcraft, arrested, tortured to make them confess and held in prison under terrible conditions before being tried and sentenced without access to counsel, witnesses or appeal.

Trials took place in towns and villages throughout the Province of Massachusetts Bay around this time but the most infamous occurred in Salem, a name meaning *peace* from the Arabic *salaam* and the Hebrew *shalom*.

People will tell you that the Puritans came to America to escape religious persecution in England. In fact, Puritans came here to establish communities where they could practice their own form of worship away from what they saw as the taint of other sects. They wanted greater 'purity' of doctrine and worship, and greater piety.

Far from having been persecuted in England, they had long resented what they perceived as the slowness of change under Queen Elizabeth I and subsequently King James I. They thought the Church of England too tolerant of practices they associated with the Roman Catholicism which Protestantism had replaced as the national religion. Their zeal, and the extent of their desired reform, was not shared by the majority of their countrymen, who did not want fundamental changes to their Book of Common Prayer (the forms of Anglican services and worship still used today) or the way the Church was governed (by abandoning bishops and making every congregation autonomous).

English Protestantism had developed from the teachings of Germany's Martin Luther. The Puritans' inspiration was the Geneva church of French theologian, John Calvin, who favoured a far more rigid religious practice than Luther. For instance, they wanted no kneeling or crossing in church, which they condemned as popery; no music apart from unaccompanied hymn-singing; no dancing, no Christmas or Easter holiday celebrations, no toys and no schooling beyond religious practice and the Bible.

They were so strict that they received criticism from non-Puritans for the harsh treatment they inflicted on their own members. In fact, an element in what happened in Salem was a lack of any outside interference. There were no voices from a wider, mixed community warning that what they were doing - such as whipping fellow-Puritans for holding a different opinion or executing them for adultery - was excessive.

Nor did the Puritan idea of freedom of worship extend to other faiths. Not only Catholics were banned from the colony but also Protestants who were not Puritans, with four Quakers being hanged in Boston for standing up for their own beliefs.

Salem had been established in 1626 and the settlement had lived peaceably for decades thanks to the benign influence of its founder. But by 1692 it was mired in clan feuds, property and boundary disputes, and bad feeling between Salem Town (present-day Salem) and Salem Village (now called Danvers) eight miles away. There were also congregational disagreements, with the Village even refusing to have the same minister as the Town and appointing its own.

Two people seem to have been crucial to what happened. One of them was an ordained minister, the influential Cotton Mather from the province's capital, Boston, who saw Satan and his cohorts lurking behind every tree. The other was the like-minded William Stoughton – a major landowner, colonial magistrate and administrator – who had just been appointed the province's Lieutenant Governor on the recommendation of the Reverend Cotton Mather.

There was also Samuel Parris, the minister recently engaged by Salem Village. However, far from calming the turbulence in his new parish, he made it worse by constantly harrying his flock over petty infringements. According to many sources it was in the Reverend Mr Parris's home that the situation took a tragic new direction.

His 9-year-old daughter and 11-year-old niece began having fits, screaming and contorting their bodies into strange shapes. With the local doctor finding no medical cause, demonic possession was suggested. Soon their school friends began having fits too. In no time at all, adults announced themselves under attack by witches as well. And although in England witchcraft trials had ended a decade earlier - thanks to The Enlightenment and the ideas of Humanism percolating through Europe – in Salem, accusations of witchcraft were still rampant.

The first to be accused were the usual suspects: aging women, non-conformists and outsiders. Bridget Bishop, the first to die, was sixty years old. Her poor church attendance, the cut of her coat and the colours she wore offended Lieutenant Governor Stoughton's sense of what befitted a Puritan. She was sent for trial at the beginning of June and hanged a week later. But it wasn't long before covenanted members of the church found themselves being hauled into court as well.

The process of determining guilt, as defined by Cotton Mather, was essentially that demons are evil, but if you don't believe in demons you can't believe in angels, and if you don't believe in angels you must be evil. Denying the existence of demons, and thus being unable to have had congress with them, was no defence against the charge of being a witch.

He also introduced spectral evidence, which meant that if someone claimed to have seen your shape, or spectre, afflicting them (with fits, a failed crop, an infant death or a sick farm animal) then you must have given the Devil permission. Ergo, you were a witch.

All anyone had to do to punish a neighbour for a perceived slight, or lay claim to their property, was to go to a magistrate and make a complaint. The accused was often brought to court the same day.

Some refusing to admit their guilt were 'pressed', that is placed under a board which then had more and more rocks piled onto it until either the person underneath confessed or was crushed to death. If you confessed you could escape hanging, but a confession of guilt meant that your property would be confiscated, leaving your dependents destitute. Nor was execution the end of it. A decent burial was denied you and you were excommunicated.

Giles Corey, a farmer and a respected church member, showed his contempt by refusing to recognise the court. Although his property had already been confiscated he still refused to confess and was pressed, despite being over eighty years old. After two days he died, still protesting his innocence. Four year old Dorothy was the youngest to be arrested. Interrogated by the court, her answers were construed as evidence of her mother's guilt as well. Dorothy was imprisoned and her mother hanged.

A major element in the madness seems to have been the lack of a steadying hand. Sir William Phips, the new Governor and a humane man, had hurried away to a border war in Maine. In his absence, the very people who should have prevailed appear to have been the ones driving the hysteria to greater heights. The clergy kept inventing new 'proofs' of guilt which were impossible for the accused to refute, while the magistrates kept issuing warrants despite their dubious legality.

Lieutenant Governor Stoughton, in the conflicting roles of Chief Justice, Chief Judge *and* Prosecutor, could have put a stop to it but instead presided over a court which found everybody guilty. One jury did actually acquit a defendant, Rebecca Nurse, but Stoughton told them to go back and think again and they returned with a guilty verdict.

The trials were quickly brought to an end when Governor Phips returned from the fighting. The magistrates at least had the grace to be ashamed, and the judges to feel they had gone too far. All except one man who acted in both roles. He was John Hathorne, an ancestor of the 19th century novelist Nathanial Hawthorne whose novels about New England Puritans David and I have been reading.

The author added a 'w' to his name to dissociate himself from his unrepentant predecessor, who entered the history books as The Hanging Judge due to his enthusiasm for sentencing people to death. Sir William Stoughton also repented nothing and, following Sir William Phips' untimely death, acted as Governor.

So what was at the bottom of it all?

Initially the satanic element, so foreign to modern sensibilities, diverts the attention. But much analysis has been devoted to the Salem tragedy as a way of understanding subsequent conflicts and a depressingly familiar motive soon begins to emerge: namely, self-interest.

Cotton Mather was a prolific writer of books, tracts and pamphlets (around 450 of them) before, during and after the trials and the driving force of much of his penmanship was a desire to return second- and third-generation Puritans to their theological roots. Along with other members of the colony's clergy, he saw the trials as a way of returning backsliders to the fold and reasserting Puritan authority in the province. It was an ambition shared by Lieutenant Governor Stoughton.

The magistrates appear to have been the willing tool of the clergy in drawing up arrest warrants, although a factor no doubt was the fear that a refusal to sign a warrant could put you on the next cart to Gallows Hill. Similarly the judges, many of whom had no legal training and relied on Cotton Mather to advise them on what made a person guilty of witchcraft.

Many of these prominent men, because of their position in society, had been responsible for protecting the province's frontier against Indian raids. Unfortunately they had made a poor job of it, which was why

Governor Phips was away fighting a border war in Maine. It had also produced large numbers of refugees, whose presence had contributed to the social unrest in Salem and elsewhere. These witchcraft trials, it has been argued, were a way of deflecting criticism from their own military failures onto the spiritual lapses of their inferiors. And, of course, there was all that valuable confiscated property to be redistributed.

Inevitably present-day Salem lives up to its past with lots of Halloween and witch-themed attractions, shops and Wiccan boutiques. The name of the local elementary school is Witchcraft Heights, the high school's athletic teams are called The Witches and the town's police patrol cars carry a logo of a witch on a broomstick.

There are also a number of historic buildings along the waterfront, and ten minutes' walk away is the historic district. Nathaniel Hawthorne, born in Salem in 1804, spent part of his childhood in a gabled house there. It belonged to a cousin of his and, along with her stories of their Puritan ancestors, inspired his novel *The House Of The Seven Gables*.

However, it is in *The Scarlet Letter*, generally accepted as Hawthorne's finest work, that he confronts Puritanism head on. And having finished reading it, both the witch trials and the novel fall into place.

Both communities have at their core a powerful elite which ignores a belief in God's grace and the principle of redemption in favour of religious discipline and ideas. Or, put another way, it elevates the letter of the law above its spirit and the theological term for this is legalism.

In Salem, such was the obsession with bringing the congregation into line with ideas of how people should dress, behave and worship that even common humanity was abandoned, let alone Christian love and forgiveness.

In the 17ᵗʰ century Boston in which Hawthorne's novel is set, the letter of the law actually takes on physical form, as a large embroidered capital A for Adultery, which Hester Prynne must wear on the front of her dress as a public mark of her shame.

With our outboard motor out of commission we have taken the water taxi into Salem today and something the driver tells us is that the Shackleton exhibition currently in town is well worth a visit. How could anyone resist immersing themselves in one of the most inspiring sailing adventures ever? Our priority at present, though, is to do something about *Voyager*'s undercarriage.

50
Voyager is Lifted Out

The first boatyard we try is a long walk from Salem Harbour towards the end of town only to find that its lift isn't wide enough. We wish the man now informing us of this had answered the enquiry we'd left on his answer-phone and saved us this foot-blistering walk. I sit on a low wall outside his office and put plasters on my heels before setting off for the next yard on our list.

It is called Riley's Yacht Yard although it seems to be used mostly for fishing boats. As we enter we are glared at by three seventy-somethings in polo shirts, shorts and baseball caps, sitting in a row on a wooden pallet. All three are short, portly and two of them are smoking fat cigars. The one in the middle rises slowly.

'Lookin' for somebody?'

Mick Riley, owner, Irish-American, full volume, aggressive. Nothing personal, it's how he conducts all his conversations. He can lift *Voyager*, the price is reasonable, and we arrange a time. Although what we hadn't realized until now is that the creek between Salem Harbour and the boat yard contains a fixed bridge which is only 49 feet high at Median High Water. However, given the 9ft drop in the tide and with a little planning we shall be able to manage.

Next morning we time our departure to arrive at the bridge with the tide just low enough for us to sneak under it while there is still enough water beneath our keel to stay afloat during the rest of the journey. Once under the bridge a fisherman draws alongside, asks where we are going and says, 'Follow me'.

We get so far, but unfortunately there are crab traps and moored boats in the channel and in trying to avoid one of them we run aground. We need to wait for a bit more tide so that we can float off, but thank the fisherman for his kindness and assure him we shall be fine so that he can go back to work. We go aground several times more before we get to the yard and it ends up taking us an hour and forty minutes to do two and a half miles.

Having waited for the tide to drop so that we could get under the bridge, once we get to the yard we have to wait for it to rise enough for us to get into the travel lift. In the meantime we are tied up to a large, geriatric motor yacht which appears to do service as a club room, if the row of bottles lining the window ledge is anything to go by.

Late in the afternoon, at high tide, *Voyager* is lifted out and we are finally able to see the full extent of the barnacle infestation on her hulls. Mick's two helpers, each with a short, fat cigar clamped between his teeth, power wash *Voyager*'s bottom.

As it is late by the time they finish, Mick decides to leave us where we are in the slings and move us to a permanent spot in the morning. Then with the soft hue of a low evening sun glinting off all its different coloured bottles, the three of them repair to the elderly motor yacht.

Next morning *Voyager* is put up on blocks at just the right height for working under her. Mick drives me to Sam's Laundromat, and Sam brings me back. Meantime David begins cleaning our boat's hulls and topsides.

A local man, called Josh, stops by to offer his services in getting about. A boater himself, he had seen us coming down the creek yesterday. He had also seen our Red Ensign. 'I spent some time in England,' he tells us. 'People were nice to me.'

The retired couple across the yard also offer to take us anywhere we need to go in their van at any time. Which is very kind since their van is also their workshop. They have a classic wooden sloop from which they are laboriously stripping all its old varnish. Then they will put on twelve coats of new varnish. What they have stripped so far looks magnificent, but is a mammoth job expected to take months.

An electrician comes out to our anchor winch.

The lobster boat *Marie-Jo* is lifted out. She's hit a fishing buoy and 'torn the cotton from her hull'. And nine-year-old Lewis from an aging trawler yacht comes over to tell us about his millionaire status, his Dad's trust funds and his double joints.

Mick bawls at the boy's father, 'If ya gonna go back in, ya gotta do it soon!'

David asks, 'Is this part of your customer service initiative, Mick?'

One of Mick's helpers cackles into his fat cigar. We polish the port topsides and much of the starboard.

At dawn Sunday morning we resume polishing the starboard topside, finishing just as Josh arrives to take us to a local place for a full fried breakfast. It is heavenly.

Afterwards we start putting on the antifouling paint.

We are re-launched and re-attached to the elderly motor yacht ready for tomorrow's tide. In the meantime, the last of Josh's many kindnesses is to drive us miles and miles to buy a replacement outboard for our dinghy. You can use a 2-stroke outboard engine here, and buy one second-hand – if you can find one - but you cannot buy a new one as they are no longer made. A two-stroke's size and weight suits our lightweight dinghy but they are getting quite scarce. Josh has located a reconditioned 2hp Evinrude for us.

Next morning, while I wash the dirt of a haul-out from the decks and fill the water tanks, David goes up the mast to fix the wind speed indicator and the steaming light. From the doorway of the office on the far side of the yard Mick yells up at him, 'Would you like to pay the bill?'

David yells back: 'There's a bill?'

In the office David presents our credit card. 'Ah,' says Mick, and apologises for not mentioning earlier that he doesn't accept credit cards. Given our card's limit, to get cash from an ATM will mean staying here another three days. Fortunately our last mail envelope from home contained David's renewed driver's license and using that as ID David chats up a bank teller and acquires enough cash against our credit card to pay our bill.

Sadly, all our hard work in the boatyard does not seem to have solved another pressing problem: our expanding waistlines. In only four months David has put on eight pounds and I've gained nine. There are several reasons. One of them is availability. Our Caribbean shopping had been limited in terms of choice and thereby helped us continue the Mediterranean-style diet we had adopted on first setting out from England.

Getting to America from the British Virgin Islands had also resulted in a ten-day passage through turbulent seas which meant our bodies got little repose, even lying on our bunks, while the rest of the time was taken up keeping our balance. It acted like a perpetual exercise machine, burning off calories. Food also tends to lose some of its allure under those conditions.

So, what with the light, healthy eating followed by the inadvertent exercise regime we had arrived here as thin as reeds and then went stupid. There was the chocolate fudge cake for a start. And some really delicious old-fashioned doughnuts with red jam in the middle and rolled in sugar. And that light, very palatable American beer with those extra-large packets of crisps. And there is nothing nicer, drifting down a tranquil river on a sunny afternoon, than a little wine and cheese party. Very relaxing.

And America has a sweet tooth. According to government statistics Americans eat 150 lbs of sugar per head per year. And I have to say that, as a European, when you first arrive here you are startled by the sweetness of everything; especially those things you don't associate with it. For instance, sweet bread is fine for a jam sandwich, but not with cheese or pâté.

Initially we would wave an arm over shelves and shelves of different types of bread: white, brown, wholemeal, five-grain, eight-grain, sourdough, hard rolls, soft rolls, dinner rolls … while asking supermarket staff hopefully if one of them was less sweet than the others. *Anything* without so much sugar in it, or honey or molasses. But they would merely look puzzled. To them it was not sweet. It was normal.

And it isn't only the bread. Where else in the world would you find artificial sweeteners for your cup of coffee with equivalent strengths up to four teaspoons of sugar. Even the toothpaste seems to have sweetener in it; or at least more than you are used to. It's like cleaning your teeth with melted peppermint creams. Your taste buds soon adjust to all this sugar, of course, until you are no longer surprised by a news item that American scientists are using genetic engineering to grow sweeter pineapples.

But given that extra inches never appear in the places you'd like them, we are now *pot-bellied* reeds. Something will have to be done.

We leave Riley's Yacht Yard at slack water high tide and anchor downriver near the bridge to wait for the water to drop. We have done it this way to avoid having a strong current against us as well as all those shallow places we encountered on the way down. It is a winding river and the current plus wind over tide gives us no peace. We surge around our anchor for nearly five hours, re-anchoring twice, before the water is low enough to get under the bridge. Then we return to our original anchor spot in Salem Harbour. Our old neighbours pop over for a chat.

Monday, they tell us, is Labor Day making the coming weekend another federal holiday. So every man and his boat will be out on the water shortly and it is best to be anchored quietly out of the way in a creek somewhere if possible.

51
Summer's End

Labor Day, which takes place on the first Monday in September, celebrates the economic and social contribution of workers to the wealth of the nation. As with Memorial Day, the three-day holiday provides a large number of people with the opportunity to shop. In fact, retailers claim that it generates revenue second only to the period from Thanksgiving to Christmas.

More Americans work in the US retail sector than any other and, given the importance of Labor Day Weekend's sales figures, far from getting a day off to celebrate their contribution to national prosperity, a fair number of them will be manning the checkouts; and may even end up working longer hours than normal.

Just as Memorial Day in May had signalled the beginning of the summer vacation season, Labor Day is generally accepted to be its end. Before the holiday officially starts, however, we want to take one last trip into Salem. It will also be the maiden voyage of our new, second-hand Evinrude 2hp outboard engine and the best trip I've experienced in our dinghy for quite some time.

Not wishing to bad-mouth an old and faithful retainer, I had not realized how raddled our old outboard had become. From its replacement, however, there is little noise and hardly any vibration. I can actually see clearly while on the move now, instead of everything being a bit blurred. And David and I can even converse while on the move. I love it! The only drawback is that he starts to get electric shocks from it, although he says 12 volts are OK and if he wraps his handkerchief around the tiller it reduces the sting quite a lot. Fortunately it turns out to be only a temporary hiccup.

Salem has a policy of no dinghies. We learn this from a tugboat captain who helps us squeeze ours into a tiny space between the water taxi landing stage and the piles supporting it, which is all that constitutes a public dock. And then he lends us a piece of rope to tie up our dinghy's stern to prevent it drifting out.

Our objective is the Peabody Essex Museum and the Shackleton exhibition it is hosting, as recommended by the man operating the water taxi we used on our previous trip into town. There are some personal effects and a reproduction of the lifeboat that really was a life preserver, but the centrepiece of the exhibition is the photography of Australian Frank Hurley - mostly black and white stills, a small amount of movie film and a handful of some of the earliest surviving colour transparencies.

These images record the life and death of *Endurance* – the sailing ship that carried Ernest Shackleton's 1914-17 Imperial Trans-Antarctic Expedition - and the daily life and survival of the men aboard her. For amazingly all 28 of them survived, due in great part to the extraordinary navigation skills of New Zealander Frank Worsley and the man-management genius of Shackleton himself. The plan had been to cross the Antarctic from coast to coast via the South Pole, and is nowadays considered to be the last major expedition of a heroic age of Antarctic exploration that includes Scott and Amundsen.

After the *Endurance* was crushed by pack ice in the Weddell Sea, in the winter of 1915, Shackleton left most of his crew on Elephant Island. Then, with Worsley and four other men, he set sail for South Georgia to get help in one of *Endurance*'s lifeboats, the *James Caird*. Only 22 feet long, it had been expertly adapted for the journey by the ship's carpenter Harry McNeish, who also sailed with them

Worsley navigated it 800 miles across the South Atlantic using only a sextant, which required two men to hold him steady in the heaving sea while he got a fix on the sun and its angle from the horizon. Because of the appalling weather, Worsley was granted only six sightings of the sun during the entire voyage but still managed to arrive at the small island of South Georgia nine days later.

Once there, Shackleton, Worsley and another man from the lifeboat then crossed the mountains of South Georgia in a thirty-six hour march to the Stromness Whaling Station to arrange for the rescue of the other crew members – the three left with the *Andrew Caird* on the other side of South Georgia, and the twenty-two camped on Elephant Island. Thanks to unrelenting sea ice, the latter would remain there for four long months before a boat could reach them, but every man who set out on the expedition would eventually return home.

In a small room beside the main exhibition there is a full-size reproduction of the *James Caird* lifeboat and a re-creation of the conditions it encountered: the oppressive grey light; the fleeting emergence of the sun which was all that Worsley had to provide readings for his sextant; the roll of the small boat in the 50-foot waves they endured; and the roar of the sea and wind.

The photography is stunning, not just for its evocation of life aboard *Endurance* and on the ice pack but its extraordinary quality, especially given the cumbersome equipment of the early 1900s and the conditions under which the film was exposed, stored and transported back to England.

Frank Hurley took far more pictures than now survive. He had to make a choice, given the limited space available, and leave the rest behind. A particularly memorable one is of a great wave in a temperature so cold that the salt water has frozen solid at the very moment it curls over. Another extraordinary thing is that the sea ice is blue.

As well as all his other kindnesses to us, Josh has also told us how to get to old Salem Village, now Danvers, by dinghy. The home of one of the executed women - Rebecca Nurse, initially found innocent by the jury until Lieutenant Governor Stoughton sent them back to think again - still stands and is now a monument to the victims of Salem's witch mania. Of the parsonage, which once housed Samuel Parris and his family, only the foundations remain.

We intend to leave Salem tomorrow. We have also decided not to go any further north. We've found our American odyssey so enjoyable that we should like to do it again next year, visiting places we missed this time around and spending longer in those we especially enjoyed.

That being the case, Maine will still be there next year, and it is shrouded in fog now anyway. A yachtsman newly arrived in the anchorage says he's just spent two weeks there and never saw the shoreline once. The forecast for next week is for more of the same and there's little chance of its improving much in the long term either. Bad weather further north could hold us up and, even with an extension to our visas, there are still time constraints on us. A return south seems sensible.

Labor Day Weekend dawns cold and grey with drizzling rain. Since it is forecast to last all day we postpone our departure until tomorrow. The coastline beyond the harbour entrance gradually disappears, with the horizon reduced to a strip of silver between two shades of dark grey. No holiday boats arrive. Do the gods hate working people? If not, why is the weather the world over invariably bad on weekends and public holidays? One lone yachtsman, with the hood of his foul weather jacket resting on his nose, steers purposefully out of the harbour. It is Saturday and a holiday weekend and he is going out no matter what.

52
Provincetown

On the passage to Provincetown we have two knots more speed as a result of *Voyager*'s haul-out and she looks beautiful – positively aglow from all the polishing. It is an uneventful journey, apart from a whale-watching boat which makes a great sweeping detour to slice across our bows so that its patrons can have a look at us and which nearly bounces us off our seats. It may be a sign that they haven't found any whales today.

We anchor in Provincetown's rocky-bottomed harbour late afternoon. Soon afterwards there is a feeding frenzy off our port side. Large fish leap, while their small, frantic prey turn and turn again in their ever-decreasing shoal but never escape. It lasts an hour. Meanwhile fishermen in dinghies pull the large fish from the water only to throw them back in again. I am as underwhelmed by fishing as I am football. By which, of course, I mean English football. As for American football, I don't understand why you'd even call something football when the foot and the ball rarely come together because the players spend most of their time running about the pitch with it tucked under their arm.

We are currently reading the first book of an Arthurian trilogy we found in Salem's bookshop. All we have to do now is track down the other two volumes. I suppose we could always ask the author. He lives around here somewhere.

Labor Day itself begins with fog so thick we cannot see the town and everywhere so damp that *Voyager*'s exterior is bejewelled with moisture. We are experiencing an area of high pressure that is moving down from Canada and bringing Massachusetts an instantaneous autumn with a morning temperature of only 54°F. A sudden drop of over 20 degrees is quite a shock.

The wind that ultimately rises and disperses the fog is a cold one. It also reaches 25 knots for a while, making the water bang ceaselessly under our bridge deck. Still, it is a holiday weekend so what can one expect? And as such, people continue to do holiday things. A young woman falls from a jet ski and has difficulty hauling herself out of the frigid water and into the plunging rescue dinghy. We offer Voyager's steps for her to climb up onto first.

Men in small boats, trailing fishing rods, look pinched and irritable as they slice across our stern, and occasionally each other's lines after which a bit of shouting ensues. It is so cold and choppy, and we are such a long distance from a landing place for our dinghy, that we postpone a trip ashore.

The sea becomes increasingly rough as evening progresses. Around 10.30pm we bump onto the harbour bottom. The next half hour is spent shivering on deck hauling in chain against a 25-knot wind. It seems that the water in which we had anchored had been wind-driven, thereby providing less water under our keel at low tide than we were expecting. David lets out some more chain a few hours later but remains up all night.

With the holiday safely over the wind drops, the sun shines brightly in a cloudless blue sky and we go ashore at last. Provincetown – often shortened to P-town - is a popular tourist destination with a long-established artists' community and some impoverished fishermen - at least to judge by their boats they are. The tourist booklet talks of 'diminishing stocks'. It's surprising there's anything left at all given the amount of pots laid in every available stretch of water, the over-eating induced by all-you-can eat menus, oversize helpings ('Would you like to take that home?') and large quantities simply left on the plate. And it's not just seafood or massive servings of fries. Familiar with British and European food prices, I can't understand how anyone can produce chicken cheap enough to retail at twenty drumsticks for $2.45 or fourteen thighs for $3.15.

We go to see the Pilgrim Monument. It is located among some very pretty homes. The design of the traditional Cape Cod cottage emerged in the 17th century to withstand the storms of the Massachusetts coast. It is low and broad with a pitched roof, a central chimney, and a door with a window either side. Simple, symmetrical, and with little ornamentation, it is the stuff of many a child's drawing on a family's refrigerator door. New houses still follow this colonial pattern.

The Pilgrim Monument was built in 1910, to commemorate the first landing on 21 November 1620 of the *Mayflower* Pilgrims (not to be confused with the Salem Puritans). This was the Pilgrims' actual landing place, although their colony was founded at Plymouth across the bay.

The monument is the tall dragon tower we observed from our anchorage on our earlier visit and is, in fact, based on one in Siena.

Although nobody could say, even at the time, why a 252-foot bell tower of early 14ᵗʰ century design from Roman Catholic Italy - with no apparent connection to a Protestant English settlement in the New World - was chosen.

But from visiting many places and monuments in many countries I'd say that was not unusual. It is known as The Curse of the Planning Committee, when after months of haggling a town ends up with whatever a majority of committee members are willing to vote for.

And anyway, from the top there is a splendid view over the town and Cape Cod Bay. Not to mention the curvature of the earth.

Plymouth was the second successful English settlement after Jamestown, Virginia (1607) and became the oldest continuously inhabited one. The celebration of its first harvest in 1621 is a cornerstone of Thanksgiving, another annual federal holiday and a major event in the calendar.

Of particular significance to many Americans is that the way in which the settlement set up its own governance – known as the Mayflower Compact - provided a framework for what would ultimately become the United States of America.

According to the latest census, P-town has a higher rate of same-sex households than any other zip code in the US. Something similar relates to visitors, with the area promoted as a vacation destination of gay men and lesbians.

There are endless couples looking disturbingly alike: similar height, close-cropped hair with quiff, shorts and T-shirts, and carrying shopping bags from Dirty White Boy and the Gay Market. Or else engaged in discussion in the supermarket about which type of onion to buy and whether they'll need parsley.

They look happy. And vulnerable. And I remember so sharply being that young, yet free at last to plumb the wonders of Blue Mountain coffee beans in a world where bottled coffee essence still dominated parental larder shelves, and green gunpowder tea bore the whiff of moral decadence.

One such couple stands, shopping list in hand, before a veritable sea of peppers.

'Why are they all different prices?' one murmurs.

'And what difference does the colour make?' asks the other.

I know I shouldn't. A stranger with a foreign accent. Intruding. But so many people have eased our confusion in so many places in the last couple of years that I do anyway.

Transport costs, I say. The green ones were grown in the US so they are the cheapest; the red have been imported from Canada; and the yellow ones are the most expensive because they have come all the way from The Netherlands. The yellow are the fruitiest and the red the tastiest. The green have the strongest flavour, but if you find it makes the sauce at all bitter you can add a little brown sugar.

They blink at me and I wish I'd minded my own business. Then one of them smiles and the other says, 'Thank you, Ma'am.' And as I turn away I see they are opting for economy and a touch of brown sugar.

Outside, a sturdy matron wheels her bicycle with a pugnacious cat in a basket on the handlebars. Parents push small children in strollers, and holiday-makers flock along the piers to climb onto the dolphin and whale watcher craft.

The picturesque waterfront is a mixture of wharves, traditional houses, fishermen's sheds, commercial premises, churches and the occasional warehouse, with a tree-lined slope rising up behind. At its back, the town is encircled by sand dunes and beaches.

Early in the 20th century a young Eugene O'Neill put on his plays here, in a wooden building on one of these wharves. They were among the first to have characters on the fringes of American society and to use the vernacular, and they became part of a new movement of realism in the nation's theatre. O'Neill had worked as a sailor for a time and the sea is often a background to his work. To have the plays performed on this waterfront, with the fog rolling in and the tide lapping against the wharf, must have provided additional drama. Many of them transferred to Broadway.

We buy two lobsters, cooked while you wait, for a ridiculously low price and have them for dinner in the cockpit with tomato salad, onion bread and olives. It tastes wonderful, especially followed by coffee and something sweet from the Penney Patch Fudge and Taffy Shop in Commercial Street. Its logo, in a circle around a minor travesty of Abraham Lincoln's portrait says, 'In Fudge We Trust 1956'.

There is a beautiful, wide orange sunset.

As if it never left, but hung around the corner waiting for morning, the huge orange sun of last evening reappears to produce a spectacular sunrise. We set off soon afterwards, back to Onset where we plan to re-fuel before sailing through the night for Long Island Sound, spend a few days in New York City and then sail on to Annapolis.

It is another lovely bright sunny day, as one would expect after a raw, wet, blustery national holiday. During the last hour or so of our journey on the Cape Cod Canal the tide turns and our speed drops by several knots. Towards the end of the canal the starboard engine begins to overheat.

Instead of just stopping for fuel and moving on as planned we anchor in Onset Bay. David tries all he knows - fan belt, water pump, and so on. After that we dinghy into Onset Bay Marina, which fortunately is a Yanmar dealership, to see what their mechanic can do. They are short of berths and want us on the fuel dock at 8am to have a look at it, when the weather will be calm, as strong winds are expected later. At least, if we need parts they don't carry, the Yanmar importer for the US is based in Massachusetts, so we could have what we need within a couple of days.

David aims *Voyager* at the fuel dock next morning with our remaining engine and two of the men tie us up quickly because calm it isn't. The high winds have arrived early. The mechanic finds that the impeller has softened and the cooling system has sucked up a mass of weed through its tubes. He also gives David a lesson in how to fix the problem if it should happen again.

We spend the next couple of days sheltering from bad weather and what would be headwinds throughout the whole of our journey. Conditions are becoming increasingly erratic and David feels we should get further south as soon as possible, postponing our visit to New York City until next year. For now, the plan is to head out to sea, sail down to Cape May in a two-night passage, then through Delaware Bay and into Chesapeake.

GOING SOUTH
FOR THE WINTER

53
Annapolis in Autumn

Annapolis harbour is blustery and bright and crowded with boats. We have some work we need to do on this visit, including servicing both engines, so our plan is to avoid the bustle of Ego Alley and anchor in the upper reaches of Spa Creek instead.

It is very pretty, although fairly narrow and full of boats. There are a lot of people heading south now – *snowbirds,* Americans call them - retirees from either side of the Canadian border who prefer to spend the winter months in the warmth of Florida; or cruisers like us heading for the Caribbean or Bahamas. Annapolis will also be hosting its annual boat show in a few weeks and a lot of people are heading into town in advance of that.

We end up rather close to a jetty off the manicured lawns of an expensive-looking home with a boathouse at the water's edge. After observing our various positions through two tide changes, David pulls in another metre of chain which sets us, as squarely as humanly possible, between the jetty, a large sloop called *Opal* and the ketch *Hawkeye*. This is not so much anchoring as fitting a piece into a jigsaw puzzle.

Then the weather turns nasty. For a couple of days it pours with rain and despite physical work all morning and bowls of hot soup for lunch, one afternoon we are so cold we climb into bed for a bit, and continue our Arthurian novel. An ambitious young sorceress is boiling a human head in urine to make spells that will usurp the power of Merlin, who is dwindling towards senility. David ponders what happens to wizards in their dotage and after a bit of discussion we settle on an old wizard's home called *Dun Wizzin.*

At night *Voyager's* interior is filled with condensation, as we cannot open anything except the companionway doors without letting the rain in, but opening the doors lets in too much cold air.

Then, quite suddenly, a clear, starry night ushers in a bright, blue-sky morning. The boat gives up its web of moisture. The warmth of the sun seeps into our bones. And the river comes alive.

Dinghies are mopped out and pets resume their morning shore leave. A couple row Snuffles to the park opposite. A ginger tabby, which snuffles instead of purring and was formerly an abandoned farm cat, Snuffles is now utterly converted to life aboard except for the occasional desire to roam unfettered on green grass.

An elderly pear-shaped man putt-putters an elderly pear-shaped black Labrador with white whiskers ashore; one immobile in the bow, the other immobile in the stern.

A tiny apricot poodle teeters on the bow of a rubber dinghy and, not waiting for it to come to a halt, gives a huge leap onto its yacht's stern, takes the cockpit in two bounds and hurtles into the saloon to greet the members of the family it recently left behind. Much as a dog loves a walk, it likes it best when its pack herds together, so that it can keep an eye on everyone.

With the weather now fine, a small green tourist boat plies the river with a commentary on tape so that the words never vary. Going upstream: 'This was the last part of the river bank to be developed. It was originally a single house but it burned to the ground. The land was then subdivided, providing for the lovely homes you see now.' On its return downstream: 'These buildings were designed by (name always lost) who was also responsible for the restoration of ...' And like a litany learned by heart we are soon reciting the words along with the tape each time the boat passes.

A workman straddles the roof of the boathouse opposite and begins to repair its lantern. Below him, in the crowded anchorage, the river is not without its tensions. The owner of a recently-arrived motor yacht has left his radar turned on, its scanner rotating above the cockpit. His nearest neighbour, a sailing minimalist without so much as an outboard motor to his name, demands he turn it off. It is destroying his brain cells, he says indignantly, and his testosterone. Undaunted by this hostility towards his material superfluity, the man with the offending radar later offers us the use of his clothes dryer. 'At any time.'

After the rain comes blistering heat, in the mid-90s, but our neighbour on the sloop called *Opal* says another cold front is expected, bringing strong winds. Late afternoon, crewed by an overweight couple and a small three-legged dog, a sloop called *Baggage Claim* arrives and squeezes in between *Voyager*, *Opal* and *Hawkeye*.

At 3 o'clock next morning I am wide awake, listening to the wind getting up, the whine of wind generators and a distant clanker. But it is the drop in temperature that has woken me. The promised cold front is arriving. I close the hatch above my head, pull up the bedding and go back to sleep.

Half an hour later, in a welter of loud voices, I rear up from my pillow to see the stern of *Baggage Claim* attached to the bow of *Hawkeye*.

Hawkeye's owner works long hours, setting up and taking down for boat shows. He leaves the anchorage early, always quietly, and returns late. He is currently just a vague shape behind a small torch beam. Then a gas light in the cockpit of *Baggage Claim* is switched on, bathing everything around it in a startlingly white glare.

The couple on board tries to re-anchor but the trick with this river bottom is to drop your hook and leave it, then test it when it's had time to sink through the silt into something a bit more solid underneath. Their method is to drop their anchor and trawl backwards and forwards in the hope that it will catch onto something. It doesn't, and with sinking heart I watch them begin lurching towards us.

Anticipating mayhem in a confined space and a rising wind I get up, put on shorts and a dressing gown and go up on deck. The temperature has dropped considerably and the cold wind is particularly sharp after the 90 degree heat of the last few days. David, woken from a deep sleep, joins me.

He is staring heavy-eyed into the blinding white light at the crew of *Baggage Claim*. A few yards ahead of us they drop their anchor and begin ploughing another furrow. The anchor doesn't hold and the wind drives it directly at our bow. Only some determined work with our boat hook prevents its stern from drifting between our bows and wedging itself under our foredeck. They lift their anchor again and have just motored past *Opal* when their engine dies.

After what seems a long time the man shouts to the woman that they must have something caught around their prop and throws out his anchor again to stop their drift. We can only hope it hasn't landed on top of ours. If it has, there will be two boats trying to re-anchor in a rising wind and a very confined space. For the present they are along our port side.

'What about putting some fenders out?' the woman shouts to nobody in particular. She doesn't. But I do, because as well as their starboard quarter now threatening our topsides, their outboard motor blades are hanging over the sharp-edged wooden dinghy floating off their stern.

Placing fenders in these conditions is not a simple matter, so I am darting about with them and David is fending off with the boat hook when the man from *Opal* appears out of the darkness and wedges his inflatable dinghy as a giant fender between *Baggage Claim* and *Voyager*. Like the man from *Hawkeye*, he also works long hours, leaving early and returning late.

'I'd just got to sleep,' he says wistfully in a voice that is deep and resonant, and the last time I heard anything like it was Hoagy Carmichael singing *Stardust*. I look at the warm dressing gowns David and I are wearing and then at his thin cotton shorts and singlet. 'Can I offer you a jacket or something?' I ask him. 'This wind is rather cold.'

'Thank you, no,' he says, his words slow, polite, mellifluous. 'Actually, I'm finding this quite delightful. I've been rather too hot for several days now.'

With his dinghy, and our boat hook, *Baggage Claim* is kept at bay. In the meantime, with infinite slowness its captain puts on swimming trunks, his reading glasses and a diving mask. Then he disappears under his stern with a torch and a knife.

Each time he comes up for air he hits his head on his dinghy. *Opal*'s skipper says quietly to the man's wife, 'Why don't you pull your dinghy out of the way so he doesn't keep hitting his head on it?'

She tries, but can't shift it.

The man surfaces again. 'Can't you do something with the dinghy?' he shouts at her irritably. 'I hit my head on it every time I come up for air!'

'I'm trying but it won't move,' she says.

'What?' he says.

'The end of the painter must be caught.'

'*What?*'

I assume he is deaf until I discover later that he hears even the softest tones of the man from *Opal* perfectly well, because he always responds to what the man says. He simply chooses not to acknowledge anything his wife says until she's said it two or three times. Heaven preserve them if they ever go to sea and become involved in a real drama.

Ultimately the man decides that while he can't see underwater without his reading glasses, they are useless inside the facemask so the wife disappears into their saloon. She returns in a swimsuit complaining loudly up at us that she really doesn't want to do this. But after a lot of toe-testing, grumbling and short sharp breaths, she lowers herself in. Meanwhile, the wind drives their boat remorselessly down onto *Voyager*.

'Do you have a second anchor?' asks *Opal*'s skipper. 'To save keep pressing down on these people?'

'Yeah, somewhere,' says the man, and begins to burrow into the vast amount of clutter in his cockpit. It covers the coaming and most of the seating and is usually only seen in such quantities on very old boats that have been abandoned in marinas and not moved in years.

The man emerges with an anchor. 'Got no rope on it,' he says, plunging back in. He reverses out at last with a suitable length of rope, untangles it, ties it to the anchor and throws it over the side where it is no more effective than the one he threw over the bow.

In the meantime, her safety ignored, the woman under the stern continues to saw through the rope and bang her head on the dinghy each time she comes up for breath. Their boat continues to bear down on ours.

'Perhaps you could pull in that second anchor,' *Opal*'s captain suggests quietly.

'Sure,' says the man, and pulls his boat off us, although it immediately resumes its drift, albeit more slowly.

It is at this moment that the three-legged dog appears on deck and hobbles off towards the bow.

'Maybe it's off to do something useful with the bow anchor,' I whisper to David.

'N-no,' he says, rubbing a hand across his eyes. 'I don't think that's what it's doing.'

I squint past the blinding white glare of *Baggage Claim*'s cockpit towards its shadowy bow, and then glance away. A dog has a right to privacy like anybody else, and indeed should be congratulated. The poor creature, its sleep disturbed by all the upheaval and its morning functions stimulated beforetime, appears to be the only crew member who instinctively does what it needs to do quickly and efficiently.

'I suppose they'll notice when they go to pull up the anchor?' I say.

David sighs and pulls his dressing gown tighter around him.

The little dog makes its way back along the side deck and returns indoors. Gradually, the wind begins to fall away.

Finally the wife emerges from the water brandishing the offending rope, throws it into their dinghy with a yell of triumph and climbs back into the boat. The man tests his engine. It fires and he cheers loudly.

'Better try putting it in gear to make sure it's not damaged,' murmurs Opal's skipper, just audible above the engine noise.

'Oh yeah,' shouts the man. The gears mesh and the boat moves forward. 'It's fine!' he yells.

A soft sigh wafts up from the inflatable dinghy below us. 'I think I'll go back to bed.'

We both thank him very much. He raises a hand in a gesture which says he was protecting his own boat as much as ours but we are nevertheless very grateful to him. An aluminium dinghy makes a useless fender.

'Yeah, thanks for your help,' the captain of *Baggage Claim* shouts grudgingly as the man from *Opal* returns to his bed, with an hour left for sleep before the start of his working day. I am keen to return to my bed, too. Then I notice *Baggage Claim*'s dinghy. It has a rope trailing into the water from its bow.

'Should I mention that?' I ask David. He sighs.

The man on *Baggage Claim* slowly pulls in his second anchor, takes the wheel and revs his engine. The woman begins to make her way forward to the bow anchor. The wind has fallen away completely now. The lights from the houses and the jetties still glow silver against the dark water but, in the sky, day is approaching. The river is still and silent apart from the idling engine as the man waits for his wife to raise their bow anchor.

'*Shit!*' the woman shrieks at the top of her voice. 'I've just trodden in shit!'

But at last the anchor is raised and they prepare to move away. Limping down their side deck on befouled feet she looks at me accusingly. 'What else can go wrong?' she demands.

She has given me an opening so I fill it. 'There's a rope hanging off the bow of your dinghy,' I tell her. 'You don't want to do all this again.' No more do I. Two hours of standing in a cold wind is enough for one night.

'There's a rope hanging out of the dinghy!' she bawls at her husband although they are only a couple of feet apart.

'What?' he bawls back.

'A rope!' she yells angrily. 'It's the one I just cut free and threw in there!'

'*What?*' he yells back at her.

Neither of them attempts to remove the rope from its proximity to their propeller. They simply motor towards *Hawkeye*, drop their anchor and plough a furrow.

'*Too close!*' she yells from the bow.

'*WHAT?*' he bellows from the helm.

They finally abandon *Hawkeye* and begin circling *Voyager* hopefully instead. David and I groan in unison as we contemplate our anchor being lifted and joined with theirs and us drifting *a deux* onto one of the jetties that we have so carefully avoided for several days.

Then, without warning, the event most longed for occurs. They set off downstream and are lost from sight. And sound. We set off back towards our warm bed.

'I've never seen so much junk on a boat that moves before,' says David. 'No wonder the dog lost a leg.'

'It's probably still in there,' I yawn.

'What?' he says.

'Oh, don't you start!' I snap at him.

During the day dinghies sidle up to ask what the hell was going on last night. And the skipper of *Hawkeye* calls across to us during the evening to say it had taken him ten minutes to wake them up after they first collided with his bow.

54
Quiet Creeks and Tranquil Places

After leaving Annapolis we make a detour out of Chesapeake Bay each evening into a river or creek to anchor for the night. We could stop in more convenient places but the sheer beauty and tranquillity of these secluded anchorages is well worth an extra mile or so to spend the evening as a solitary yacht in an idyllic landscape.

We are also enjoying fresh, bright Autumn days, a little shorter now but blessedly free of rain and with the smell of wood smoke in the air. One morning we turn off the Little Choptank River into picturesque Slaughter Creek, because the guide book says it is the only place on the eastern shore to get groceries. We edge our way up a very narrow channel, anchor and dinghy into a small marina. Its pontoon is very high and only as you scramble blindly up onto it do you discover that the ducks have been there before you.

A local man, working on his boat, points out the marina's washroom and tells us that the grocery store is actually on the opposite bank, but by the time we return with clean hands he has brought his car over and offers to drive us there.

His name is Jed and I ask my usual question, but he doesn't know how Slaughter Creek got its name. 'Perhaps it has to do with the British,' he says. 'There is a little canon called Becky, taken from a British ship, rusting away across the river on the way to the shop. And the guest house behind the marina here has the same name.'

We compliment him on the beauty of the area. He slaps the back of his neck, wipes away the dead insect and quotes James A Michener, where the author says that God gave this land mosquitoes so that the people would still have an incentive to get into heaven. He says at least there are less of them since they started spraying.

'A few years ago you would wipe them off your arm by the dozen. Now everybody's afraid of West Nile Virus.'

On the journey to the store Jed tells us the current week is bow and arrow deer hunting, and the previous weekend had been black powder (flint locks). The duck season has started and they will also be shooting Canada geese. I'm beginning to see where Slaughter Creek might have got its name.

At least there is some sort of control nowadays. Michener describes a time when the slaughter of geese and ducks on Chesapeake reached massacre proportions through the use of the punt gun, so called because it was too heavy, and its recoil too great, for a human shoulder and had to be bolted onto a punt.

Used in the 19th and early 20th centuries for the commercial harvesting of waterfowl, as well as private sport, these enormous guns had a 2-inch bore and fired over a pound of shot at a time. With a single shot capable of killing fifty birds or more resting on the water's surface, and hunters working in fleets of punts, stocks of waterfowl became so depleted that the practice was ultimately banned. Even so, hunters played cat-and-mouse with the authorities for years, hiding the massive guns in the marshes and continuing to use them at night, until the last one was finally tracked down and confiscated.

There is a sanctuary nearby for geese, Jed tells us, with corn grown for them on their flight path. Food they need for their journey without devastating local crops.

'But they like it here,' he says, 'and with the winters getting milder they don't migrate anymore.'

So the shoot is to kill off a few of the residents before the next migration arrives. The numbers are so great, he says, that the golf course is virtually unusable now. And a nearby field will have 50,000 snow geese on it come migration time.

'It's so completely white,' he says, 'it looks like it's snowed.' Apparently the birds still form skeins in readiness for migration, but don't actually go anywhere.

When we reach the opposite bank we enter a store which still has a Western Union Telegraph sign on the door. Inside it is part grocery, part hardware, and part junk shop, with a counter for fishermen to fill their sandwich box and a corner for coffee and pie. It probably hasn't changed much since the 1930s.

Back out on the Little Choptank River we slip past the oystermen working from their small boats. Chesapeake Bay is the largest oyster-producing body of water in the US, although the beds have been much reduced through overfishing, disease and pollution.

To give an idea of the sheer size of the catches once taken annually from these beds, for national consumption, at their peak in the 1884/85 season the watermen hauled up 15 million bushels.

There were two methods of harvesting them. The main one was dredgers which scoured the bottom of the bay thereby destroying the beds in the process. While in shallower waters a manual method called tonging was used.

In order to preserve stocks, dredging became illegal in anything except traditional engine-less sailboats like those we watched from the marine museum carrying tourists at St Michaels. The men out here today are using tongs, like those on the walls of the Solomans Island museum. They are standing on the edge of their boats with a long-handled implement resembling two hinged rakes. When the handles are pushed together at the top, the long tines at the bottom mesh together, forming what is called a box and scooping up the shellfish. The oysterman then lifts the tongs and swings his catch aboard.

It is a back-breaking job and the oyster season includes the worst of the winter weather. It is also dangerous since the shallow water in which they work often becomes much choppier in high winds than deep water does, and these watermen spend their days perched on the edge of what is sometimes a severely rocking boat.

With regard to Chesapeake's fishing industry you become well used to the multitude of crab pots that you have to navigate daily. But one evening as we approach the Great Wicomico River, for a night in Mill Creek, we find ourselves zigzagging past a greater than usual number of another obstacle common to the Bay - fish traps.

Around fifteen feet square, fish traps comprise poles driven into the water; ropes tied around the poles; and netting attached to the rope to create an enclosure. There is also a cunning design below the water so that the fish, once they swim in, are unable to get out again. We had initially assumed the idea was that watermen would appear at regular intervals and harvest the fish, although we have never seen anyone emptying the traps. Instead, there is a look of neglect about them and some, like these today, have their netting torn, their ropes trailing and have clearly been abandoned. However, they do provide an excellent facility for the bird population which sits patiently waiting for the next contribution to their all-day buffet to show up.

Today there are cormorants and seagulls on virtually every trap, staring expectantly down into the water. The seagulls sit on top of the poles while the cormorants keep a shaky foothold on the sagging ropes between them, sometimes at comical lopsided angles.

These fish traps will sometimes extend from near the shore to as much as half a mile out into the Bay. So, to reach the creeks where we sequester each night, while David steers I stand on the bow and plot a course for him between the fish traps and the crab pots scattered among them. More than a few of the latter have also been abandoned by their owners. The buoy which should warn of its presence often lies just below water level because its rope has become too short, and with the buoy itself discoloured by weed it is often invisible from the helm. Especially with sunlight glinting off the water into the helmsman's eyes.

Mill Creek is well worth the effort, however. It is *very* beautiful in the late afternoon light. Still and silent, the trees feathery and just beginning to turn red. And half-hidden among them, a solitary house painted white. Simple. Tranquil. And in the morning, birdsong.

Another memorable detour is Mobjack, also in Virginian waters. Near the entrance to Mobjack Bay there are several more old fish traps including a broken one with its netting gone. Nevertheless, every surviving pile supports a cormorant. One stands with out-stretched wings, offering up its chest and flight feathers to the warming sun, its head turned to one side and looking for all the world like the standard of an ancient Roman legion. Another sits on its feet, resting its lower body directly onto the pole for balance, and trailing a languid wing.

And there are pelicans. It is a joy to be back among them and, as usual with them, they are doing something unexpected. I mean, for a pelican to perch on such comparatively thin rope as that strung between fish trap poles is nothing short of a triumph given their size and their great webbed feet. However, they are not simply clinging on, but actually sitting on the rope with every indication of comfort and repose. Occasionally the angle of your vision and the sunlight on the water make the rope invisible and the pelicans appear to hover, seated but unsupported, in midair.

Mobjack Bay is seven miles long and currently scattered with fishermen lifting crab traps. At the top there are four tributaries. We enter the smallest, the East River, sailing past Mobjack village - the whiteness of its church standing out against the dark of the trees - and the remains of the old steamboat wharf.

Mobjack was once a prominent town and a stopping place for the steamboats between Norfolk and Baltimore. Now its waterfront is a place of such stillness you can feel your breathing slow.

We anchor between two shoals in a small inlet off the river's channel. There's a tiny beach sloping up from the water towards tall trees, a couple of houses and, just visible between them, a field of maize.

The afternoon light does something magical to the colours, the still water reflects it back and the effect is like finding yourself in a watercolour painting. Then comes a blissful evening filled with a red-gold sun. After nightfall, a sky filled with stars.

55
Back on the ICW

The days grow colder and we are not sorry to be returning south for the winter. We have now left Chesapeake Bay and crossed that dotted line on the chart - between the Norfolk and Portsmouth banks of the Elizabeth River - which forms the beginning of the Intracoastal Waterway.

At Portsmouth we anchor off Hospital Point again. Out in the river, some naval personnel are involved with four tugs - a children's entertainment. One tug bears a huge cartoon face – a sort of Thomas the Tank Engine, American-style, but called Theodore and wearing a baseball cap - and we see our first fireboat actually hurling water around. I open a new box of teabags. A label inside says they are kosher. Some tall ships arrive and late afternoon one of them wheels about the bay firing its cannon.

Life afloat is rarely without interest. How else could you enjoy an afternoon with Theodore the Tug, a 19th century three-masted warship wreathed in smoke, a working fireboat and kosher tea all without moving from your seat?

And so we begin to retrace our course of early summer down the ICW. Its banks were green then. Now the marshes and woodland are beginning to assume their autumn finery. The trees are spattered with red and gold. The marsh grass has taken on earth colours - umber at root level, then drab green rising to ochre, with its seed heads floating in a sienna haze across the top. Although now and then, catching it from a certain angle, the sun will turn it all to gold like a field of ripened wheat.

There is little traffic on the waterway now and apart from negotiating the bridges the days are largely given up to enjoying the scenery. What really fills the senses, however, is the beginning and end of these glorious autumn days and the anchorages where we spend them.

One morning, just before sunrise, I go outside to look at Virginia's Blackwater Creek and find the world transformed into layers of colour. The reeds form a line of brown, the trees a strip of green. The sky is streaked in blue and pink and yellow, with all of them repeated in the still water until a huge quivering sun rises above the horizon and hurls a blinding shaft of gold through it all.

In North Carolina's Broad Creek one night, unable to see out because the windows are opaque with dew, I go up on deck. The blazing starlight, filling every part of the sky right down to the horizon, is being reflected in the black water around me and I stand there in the stillness and darkness wrapped in a cocoon of stars.

While heading for the floating pontoon bridge at Sunset Beach one morning - the pretty one with the tender's hut and the striped awnings on it - we become aware of two fishing floats clanking together and apparently following us.

Two grumpy old men in a dinghy arrive and admit that they habitually lay two weighted nets in the channel here, but at a depth which allows boats to go over them without harm, they say. Nevertheless, the north-bound tug which just passed us has, quite unawares, carried off one of their nets and dislodged the other one. We are currently towing it, and its floats, behind us.

David and the two men spend some time hauling rope, net and floats from around our starboard rudder while I use the port engine to keep us from damaging people's jetties and warn passing boats of an obstacle in the water.

The bridge opens only on the hour and we had been expecting to reach it in good time for the next opening. By the time *Voyager* is finally free again we seem sure to miss it. We get no apology from the two old men. On the contrary, they seem resentful at what they see as our part in the wrecking of their second net of the morning. Not a little resentful ourselves, we set off expecting a long wait at the old wooden bridge. But when it comes into view it is still open and we sail through. It has broken down and no-one knows when they will be able to shut it again.

We glide gently into South Carolina's crisp, bright blue days, cool in the shade of the genoa but warm out in the sun. Just the conditions, it seems, for being out in a small boat with a rod and line.

In fact, looking at them all, you wonder if the male population around here does anything else. At times they become a safety hazard, fatally attracted as they are to bridges, and it is not unusual to approach one with anything up to thirty small boats clustered under it.

Each boat will contain between two and four anglers of all ages and all with a general reluctance to move for anyone wanting to pass through. They turn their faces slowly up towards the yacht bearing down on them with a look that says: *But why would you want to go anywhere?* Although they do tend to get a bit of a move on when they see a barge coming.

The hunters are heard rather than seen. Except for two close inshore in their camouflage fatigues and flat-bottomed boat, trawling up and down calling for a hound which has gone AWOL in the marshes and refuses to be found.

These are unforgettable days, sometimes with a fine grey mist hovering over the water like smoke when you set off in the mornings; sometimes cleaving to the bank and making it shimmer, like a mirage.

And there are increasing numbers of birds now: not just pelicans and cormorants but graceful darters and common grackles with their white eyes. We also spot a couple of osprey, the first we have seen in several months. They live year round in Florida, it seems, winter as far up as South Carolina, but only nest further north.

On a wide stretch of water, a group of dolphins form into a semi-circle and drive a shoal of fish towards the bank, stranding them in the shallows. Then the dolphins hurl themselves at the fish and begin to feed.

On another stretch two pelicans appear to be dive-bombing a solitary dolphin close to shore, although I can't believe pelicans would ever be so boorish. It turns out that both species are simply homing in on the same shoal of fish, the pelicans probably alerted to its presence by the feeding dolphin.

Once in a while we will leave the ICW and follow a recommended 'pretty route' such as Georgia's winding Brickhill River, also said to be very popular with alligators. On the bank there are a number of canoeists just rising from their camp. We have visions of hooded eyes watching them from the marsh grass. Further along, we anxiously watch some rowers in one-man skiffs or, as gators might consider them, lunch.

We follow the drama of a Pan-pan on the VHF – out at sea a man has fallen overboard. A plane is quickly on the scene and soon afterwards the Coast Guard announces that the man has been found, but not whether he is alive or not.

By the time we reach Florida we are back into serious warmth and can understand why people from the north are so keen to retire here; except when we pass a large residential building with upwards of sixty turkey vultures circling its roof. It gives a certain *frisson* to the words, God's Waiting Room.

And, of course, the climate here tempts a lot more leisure boats onto the water. They remind us that a boat's name is more than just for registration and identification purposes. It makes a statement. A large, grand-looking motor yacht is called *Glory*. A modest one, *Anxiety*. Some are word-play, like *Midas Well*. Might as well? Or: I need to be a very rich man to fill the hole this boat creates in my bank balance? One name leaving little room for doubt is *Emotional Rescue.*

The most enigmatic we shall ever see is *Sentimental Hygiene* while some of the most inconsiderate people we ever encounter are off a boat called *Integrity*. It comes as no real surprise that one called *Compromise* has a For Sale sign on it, and perhaps a name to avoid is anything starting with the word 'Proud'. The owner of *Proud Susan* can be heard on the VHF for quite some time one afternoon pleading for a tow company to come to his assistance. And with a charge of $150 an hour this is another good reason for having two engines.

At a fuel dock we have paid for our diesel and are simply waiting for a very slow-running tap to finish filling our water tanks. A man from a nearby boat comes over. Like many Americans who see our Red Ensign or hear our accents he is curious about where we are from. He also asks how we are enjoying the ICW and we tell him it is wonderful, especially the wildlife which we had never imagined would be so prolific. He asks if we've seen any manatees. We say mostly at a distance, and usually just a nose and a tail as they tend to rise and sink in a single movement.

He looks at us sideways and gives a little half-smile. Then lifting the water hose out of our tank he says he is just going to wash this little bit of dock here at his feet - just washing this bit of dock as it is a little dirty, you understand. It being unlawful to touch, feed or give water to a manatee.

And we watch in fascination as two manatees rise up where the water trickles over the pontoon's edge. They open their strange mouths and drink with enormous pleasure for a few moments before the man returns the hose to our tank, one of them with a flipper over its companion's shoulder so they can both get their mouths under the tap water at the same time.

Almost before we know it, we are back at Fort Lauderdale where our journey began. There is a fair bit to do before setting off for the Bahamas. The usual things: call at the main post office to collect our mail, buy some computer ink cartridges and paper, and stock up thoroughly on food and the kind of domestic supplies that other boaters have been kind enough to recommend. A berth will make life easier than anchoring so we opt for the municipal marina at Cooley's Landing.

To get there you leave the ICW and turn down the New River. It is narrow, twisting and suburban and for a while we are not sure we are in the right place. With all our attention lavished on the chart and the route ahead of us, we are startled to discover that an enormous paddle steamer is tailgating us. We also discover that when we had switched off our VHF for a few moments some miles back, because of its intolerable squawk, we forgot to turn it back on again and have been talking to a number of bridges and the paddle steamer on a dead radio.

We should be more than happy to let the huge tourist boat overtake us but for the time being this is not an option. So it wears us like a mascot through the twists and turns of this busy river while we join its patrons in listening to its river commentary, including the bit which tells us that one of the buildings we pass is the State Penitentiary where 'even the prisoners get a waterside view.'

By the time we reach Cooley's Landing the river banks have become tree-lined and pretty. From our berth can be heard a distant wail and the clanging of bells as trains make their way across Fort Lauderdale. It has been said that for an American male one of the most seductive sounds in the world is that of a locomotive whistle disappearing into the distance. This is because it evokes in him dreams of the hobo, the boxcar and the endless freedom promised by this country's vast landscape.

On one of our trips back to the boat we are held up at the railroad level crossing responsible for the wailing horn and clang of bells that we can hear from the marina.

The current train is being pulled by three diesel engines. Behind them, I count 107 wagons, most with a loaded weight of over 80 tons. The last seven are flatbeds bearing the trailers from articulated lorries, or semi-trailers as they are called here. The speed of the train can only be described as stately so it takes quite a time for it to go through.

Its sheer size is awe-inspiring, as you stand there in the middle of the street with it passing only yards away; so is the way it dominates, demanding attention; the crossing bell clang-clanging continually, bringing traffic and pedestrians and everything else around it to a halt in this busy part of town. And the whistle, intermittent, telling everything in its path to get out of the way.

56
Reflections

Finally stocked, provisioned and refuelled, and with the same promise of unlimited spaces ahead of us as those evoked by a locomotive's whistle, we set off upon the open sea.

Ahead of us lie The Bahamas. Behind our stern the Florida coastline is disappearing into the haze. Settling once more into the rhythms of an offshore passage, I reflect upon our original desire to discover something of the real America, beyond the image that many of us abroad have of this very large and powerful country.

Something we hadn't given any thought to, before coming here, were the links between Britain and America through our shared history. America for us was a foreign country. But sailing up the east coast these last few months we have been reminded repeatedly of our own history and its relation to America's present: from the *Mayflower* Pilgrims and their vision of government, to the WWII veterans populating the cities and small towns of America for whom wartime Britain is part of their own personal and family histories.

America, of course, is predominantly viewed through the prism of its entertainment industry. And given that so much US drama seen abroad involves violent assaults, bad mouthing and bad attitude it was almost inevitable that those learning of our destination would say, 'But people will snarl, "Have a nice day," at you, and you'll get mugged, or worse.' Because nobody makes films and TV programmes in which people are consistently courteous, kind and helpful.

Not that America is alone in that but at least when it is your own you can recognize the difference between reality and fiction. And something it is not easy to know about America from the other side of an ocean is the sheer niceness of ordinary Americans on their home soil. Far from being aggressive, violent or criminally disposed, the people we have met in this Millennium Year *have* been consistently courteous, kind and helpful.

Total strangers have gone beyond patiently giving directions or polite greetings. They have taken us home to dinner, put us on the right bus, given us lifts, lent us their car, set up loyalty cards to save us money on our one and only visit to that particular store and offered us the use of their clothes drier. They have, in short, made us feel immensely welcome and very safe.

Nor has the reason we originally came - the accessibility and variety of the inland waterways of the Atlantic coast – disappointed. The woodlands and wildlife, grasslands and marshes, islands, seashores, capital cities, historic towns and quiet villages through which we have drifted these past months have been a delight, with some of the places visited ranking among our happiest sailing experiences ever.

Sadly, by this time next year, Americans will be struggling to come to terms with the aftermath of 9/11 and for them nothing will ever be the same again.

Glossary for Non-Sailors

Antifouling – paint put on the hull below the water line to deter marine growth and shellfish which reduces the speed of the boat.
Autopilot – device to hold the boat on a set course automatically.

Barque and Barquentine – the designation relates to the sail plan although individual ships vary within it. Basically, however, with vessels of three or more masts, a **full-rigged** ship has square sails on all its masts; a **barque** is square-rigged on just its fore and main mast; while a **barquentine** is square-rigged on its foremast only. The sails on their other masts are fore-and-aft which are easier to set. The purpose was economic. The fewer the square sails a ship carried, the smaller the crew it needed to set them, while the vessel's performance was not significantly less than that of a full-rigged ship.
Barrier Island - a long, broad sandy island lying parallel to a shore, which has built up through the action of sea and wind and which protects the shoreline from erosion.
Beam – the widest part of the hull.
Blue water cruising – long-distance ocean sailing.
Boom – a hinged pole attached to the mast which holds the bottom of the main sail and allows it to be set in various positions to catch the wind.

Clear in – like all foreign visitors, yachtsmen have to clear in with Customs and Immigration on arrival and clear out when they leave.
Coaming – raised edge on deck which helps prevent water entering the cockpit.

Davits – two small hoists to lift and hold a dinghy, usually at a boat's stern.

Gash bag – all refuse (gash) on board is bagged and taken ashore for appropriate disposal.
Gelcoat – the hard shiny outer layer covering the fibreglass from which our boat is built.
Genoa – the large sail in front of our mast.

Hard standing – the ground on which a boat rests when it is lifted out of the water to allow work to be done on its hull.

Knot – one knot equals a nautical mile covered in one hour and is roughly equivalent to 1.15mph.

Lines – ropes. See also Mooring line.

Monohull – a conventional yacht has a single (mono) hull; a catamaran like *Voyager* has two; a trimaran has three.
Mooring line – a rope used to tie a boat to the shore.

Nautical mile – one nautical mile equals roughly 1.15 land (or statutory) miles.

Oilies – slang for wet weather clothing from the days when the cloth or canvas, from which it was made, had to be oiled to make it waterproof.

Painter – a rope attached to a dinghy's bow to tie it up.
Port – left-hand side of a vessel looking forward.
Pulpit – a hand rail round the deck at the bow.
Pushpit – a hand rail round the deck at the stern.

Red ensign – the official flag flown by British Merchant Navy ships and British leisure boats. It has a red ground with the Union Flag in the top left-hand corner.

Quarter – either side of a vessel aft of the beam.

Sextant – instrument used for calculating your position at sea, now overtaken by the GPS.
Snubbing line – a rope used to take the tension off the winch while at anchor.
Sound – a long, broad stretch of seawater, usually parallel with the coast and forming an inlet from the ocean.
Squall – sudden increase in wind-speed, often accompanied by brief but heavy precipitation.
Starboard – right-hand side of a vessel looking forward.

Topsides – the sides of the hull above the waterline.
Trots – lines of mooring buoys.

Printed in Great Britain
by Amazon